How to Enjoy Paintings

Also by Andrew Wright

In this series:
How to Communicate Successfully
How to be Entertaining
How to Improve Your Mind
How to be a Successful Traveller

with David Betteridge and Michael Buckby:
Games for Language Learning

How to Enjoy Paintings

Andrew Wright

with drawings by the author

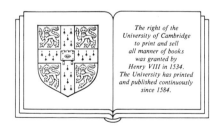

The right of the
University of Cambridge
to print and sell
all manner of books
was granted by
Henry VIII in 1534.
The University has printed
and published continuously
since 1584.

Cambridge University Press
Cambridge
London   New York   New Rochelle
Melbourne   Sydney

Published by the Press Syndicate of the University of Cambridge
The Pitt Building, Trumpington Street, Cambridge CB2 1RP
32 East 57th Street, New York, NY 10022, USA
10 Stamford Road, Oakleigh, Melbourne 3166, Australia

© Cambridge University Press 1986

First published 1986

Printed in Great Britain by
W.S. Cowell Ltd, Ipswich

ISBN 0 521 27548 2

SE

Contents

Contents

Thanks

I would like to acknowledge my teacher of art at secondary school, Mr Clarence Helliwell, my teachers at the Slade School of Art in London and particularly Professor E.H. Gombrich who helped me to understand more about the language of painting.

I would like to thank Alison Silver, the editor of this series who has made a significant contribution to each book in terms of content and presentation. I would also like to thank Monica Vincent for her valuable advice, Peter Donovan for his support during the long period of writing and Peter Ducker for his concern for the design and typography. I am also grateful to the teachers and students of Nord Anglia for trying out samples of the texts and giving me useful advice for their improvement.

In a book of this kind one is naturally influenced by a large number of writers, lecturers, friends and acquaintances. However, I should like to acknowledge the following writers and their books in particular: J.M. and M.J. Cohen, *Modern Quotations*, Penguin; *The Oxford Dictionary of Quotations*, Oxford University Press; *The International Thesaurus of Quotations*, Penguin; Ted Hughes, *Selected Poems 1957–1981*, Faber & Faber; E.H. Gombrich, *Art and Illusion*, Phaidon; Rudolph Arnheim, *Art and Visual Perception (New Version)*, University of California Press; R.W. Pickford, *Psychology and Visual Aesthetics*, Hutchinson; Will Grohman, *Paul Klee*, Lund Humphries; Paul Klee, *Pedagogical Sketchbook 1918*, translated by Sibyl Moholy Nagy, Praeger; G.T. Buswell, *How People Look at Pictures*, Chicago University Press; Bernard Shaw, *Visual Symbols Survey*, Centre for Educational Development Overseas.

About this book

How to Enjoy Paintings is one in a series of five books. There are five different chapters, each dealing with a different aspect of art and paintings; there are several different sections in each chapter. I hope you will find it all interesting, even entertaining, and that your reading of English will improve as well as your understanding and enjoyment of paintings.

★ Indicates that there is a question you should think about on your own.
★★ Indicates that if you are reading the book with another person you should talk about this particular question with him or her.

You may be reading the book while studying English in a class, with a teacher, or you may be reading it at home in the evenings, or on a train, or anywhere else – it doesn't matter!
    What I do hope is that you enjoy reading about art and paintings – in English!

Some thoughts about art

★ Do you agree with any of them?

The carpenter is preferable to the artist.

(Plato, c. 350 BC)

You use a glass mirror to see your face: you use works of art to see your soul.

(George Bernard Shaw, *Back to Methuselah*, 1921)

Art is meant to disturb. Science reassures.

(George Braque, *Pensées sur l'art*, c. 1920)

In art, as in love, instinct is enough.

(Anatole France, *Le Jardin d'Epicure*, 1895)

Thought that can merge wholly into feeling, feeling that can merge wholly into thought – these are the artist's highest joy.

(Thomas Mann, *Death in Venice*, 1913)

He is the true enchanter, whose spell operates, not upon the senses, but upon the imagination and the heart.

(Washington Irving, *The Sketch Book of Geoffrey Crayon, Gent.*, 1819–20)

Art, like life, should be free, since both are experimental.

(George Santayana, *The Life of Reason: Reason in Art*, 1905–6)

The aim of every artist is to arrest motion, which is life, by artificial means and hold it fixed so that a hundred years later, when a stranger looks at it, it moves again since it is life.

(William Faulkner, *Writers at Work: First Series*, 1958)

The world of sight is still limitless. It is the artist who limits vision to the cramped dimensions of his own ego.

(Marya Mannes, *More in Anger*, 1958)

If you ask me what I came to do in this world, I, an artist, I will answer you: 'I am here to live out loud.'

(Emile Zola, *Mes Haines*, 1866)

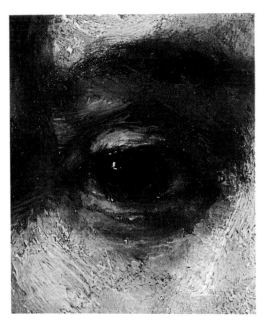

Rembrandt van Rijn (1606–1669) Detail of
'The Artist's Son Titus'
See page 43 for the complete picture.

After Pablo Picasso (1881–1973)

Art is a selection of what we see and feel

Painting is language

When we speak and when we write we represent ideas and feelings with words. In painting, ideas and feelings are represented by paint; by colour, shape and line, etc. Painting is language.

Many languages

There are many different languages in the world. There are the traditional languages of the many countries and cultures (in the United Nations headquarters you might hear up to 290 different languages!), and there are the special languages of scientists, sports lovers and others.

There are just as many styles of painting in the world. In the National Gallery in London there are about 450 pictures, painted at different periods in history and by very different people, so many of these are very different from each other.

Learning to see

We have to learn to understand and to speak a language. In the same way, we have to learn to understand a style of painting before we can begin to appreciate all its qualities . . . and what the artist is trying to say to us.

Babies have to learn to see and then learn to understand what they see. Seeing and understanding are not like breathing! They are not instinctive. When blind people have an operation in hospital they have to learn to see. At first everything is just a wild pattern of colours and light. They have to learn to see the information which tells them about how near objects are. They have to learn to associate the shape of a cat with what they have previously known through sound, touch and smell!

We are learning to see all the time. Someone who is learning to drive a car may see as much as the other road users, but they may not understand what is important. An experienced car driver has learnt to understand what he or she sees.

Expression

Here are the first two verses of a poem by Ted Hughes.

The Thought Fox

I imagine this midnight moment's forest:
Something else is alive
Beside the clock's loneliness
And this blank page where my fingers
    move.

Through the window I see no star:
Something more near
Though deeper within darkness
Is entering the loneliness:

Ted Hughes is describing how an idea comes to his mind as he sits at midnight in front of his typewriter. He might have written, 'A thought slowly came into my mind.' But his poetry gives us a much richer feeling of the place and the time and the mysterious way in which ideas come to us. His language has form (rhyming or near rhyming, contrasting sounds, rhythm, alliteration, etc.) and Hughes illustrates his ideas with rich and moving details and metaphors.

Painting is like poetry: it has form. This form can be used to represent things we recognise, but it can also be used to express ideas and feelings in the same way as poetry.

This book is about the language of painting. It is an introduction to the ways in which artists have used visual forms; shape, colour, tone, line and composition to represent people, animals, objects and scenes and to express ideas and feelings about them.

Nearly all the examples of paintings given in this book are Western. This is not because I don't value Eastern art, it is because I am more familiar with Western art.

Most recognised artists in the past have been men. For this reason I have used the pronoun 'he' throughout.

This is a personal book rather than an academic book. I am a writer and a painter and I have recorded in the book some of the ideas I think are interesting . . . and I hope very much that you do too!

How to recognise illusions

Some painters play with us

William Hogarth (1697–1764) 'The Frontispiece to Kirby's Perspective' (British Museum, London)

Hogarth was the first English painter to be famous on the continent of Europe. He was famous for his humour and he used it to comment on English society. Hogarth believed that painting is a language and he produced his own 'grammar' of visual forms. (Paul Klee, 200 years later, also produced a grammar of visual forms.) The picture reproduced here is Hogarth's examination of the 'grammatical' rules of perspective and what can go wrong if the rules aren't followed. (See also page 33 for more ideas on perspective.)

William Hogarth's picture looks quite natural. We assume that we can look at it and understand it just as we might look at a real country scene and understand what we see. But it isn't a real scene, it is a picture and is in one of the languages of painting. Language can be used to deceive, and Hogarth has shown 14 things which could not happen.

★ How many can you recognise? (They are listed on page 82.)

If you have found more than two or three it is because you are familiar with the style of picture which Hogarth has used. If you have found more than ten you are a fluent reader of pictures! If you haven't found anything wrong with the picture it is because you are not absolutely familiar with this particular language of painting.

We usually expect objects to appear to be smaller and higher up the picture when they are in the distance. In this picture, however, Hogarth has drawn the sheep higher up the picture but he has made them bigger rather than smaller than the sheep which are lower down.

('Ceci n'est pas une pipe' means 'This is not a pipe'.) Magritte, who painted this picture, lived and worked in Belgium. His paintings look real for a moment, then you realise you are being tricked. And he wants you to realise that you are being tricked! He wants us to realise that we don't understand reality very well.

Notice how Magritte has used a neat 'school teacher's' handwriting. Teachers give information about the

René Magritte (1898–1967) 'The Treason of Images' (Los Angeles County Museum of Art) The title of Magritte's picture shows us part of what he thought of pictures! He used a 'naturalistic' style to make the deception more obvious. Plato preferred a carpenter to a painter because a carpenter makes 'real' objects; but

Magritte wanted to show that there is no solid reality in either paintings or in real objects.

Magritte lived all his life in a suburb of Brussels. He looked like an 'ordinary' man and he lived in an ordinary suburb. But his 'ordinary' appearance was a deception too . . . he was a genius!

world to their students. But for a surrealist painter like Magritte, this information may be wrong! What is real? The painting is there, we can touch it. (We can touch the page in this book.) But the pipe is not there; it is only a picture of a pipe. So the sentence, 'Ceci n'est pas une pipe', is true. And yet . . .

Your mind searches for meaning

Your mind wants to find shapes and recognise depth, but it is also desperate to recognise things! It searches for things to recognise and to name. And once it has recognised something it doesn't want to change.

★ What can you see in this picture? A big vase? Yes. Two trees? Well done! What else can you see?

Do you mean that you can't see four faces? This picture secretly showed the portraits of Louis XVI and Marie Antoinette of France. There are also two other faces, one of whom may be their son, the Dauphin. It was, of course, very dangerous to be a supporter of Louis XVI and Marie Antoinette: their heads were cut off in 1793.

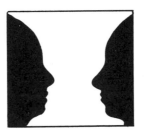

Can you see the vase *and* the two faces? If you can, good! But it is very difficult to see the vase and the two faces at the same time. We look. We try to recognise and when we have recognised something we don't want to change our minds!

After a Royalist print from the French Revolution (c. 1793)

5

Try these experiments

Are these lines flat on the paper or do they make a 'box of space'? Is line B in front of line C or behind line C? Are we looking under the box or on top of the box?

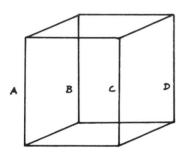

- ★ Can you see both boxes? It is difficult. The mind makes a decision about 'the truth' and then it won't change!
- ★★ Show this picture to your friends and discuss it with them. You will find how unhappy people are to accept that it is possible to see the picture quite differently.

Your mind learns to 'read' lines and shapes. Unfortunately, it can make mistakes! You might be absolutely sure you are right but be absolutely wrong!

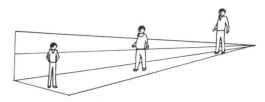

- ★ Which is the tallest man? Most people think that the man on the right is the tallest. He is not the tallest. They are all the same height! Measure them!

You have learned that lines which come together and meet at a point are going into the distance . . . not across the paper. And you have learned that people in the distance look smaller than people near you. The man on the right is drawn as big as the man on the left. He seems to be in the distance because of the lines. So you think he is a giant!

This drawing is called an 'optical illusion', a false belief of the eye. There are a lot of optical illusions. Here is another one:

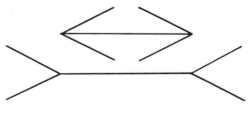

They are not just funny tricks. These illusions show us that our minds have to interpret the information they receive. We have to learn to see and understand and we can be wrong.

Most artists want us to recognise what they are describing and expressing. However, Hogarth and

Magritte wanted to remind us that paintings are paintings and not what they represent.

Can you recognise these drawings?

Several hundred peope in Kenya were shown the drawings below. They were asked to say what the drawings represent. 272 of the people lived in towns and were educated. Another 297 lived in the country; they hadn't been to school and they were illiterate. Try to 'read' the pictures yourself. See if you have any difficulty.

★ Is this a hoe or a man?

93% of the 272 people in the towns gave the correct answer. It is a hoe! However, 131 people out of the 297 who lived in the country gave the wrong answer or didn't know what to say. They knew what a hoe is but they couldn't recognise this drawing of one. Some of them thought it was an axe (perhaps they couldn't see that the blade is at right angles to the shaft). Some people thought it was a man walking along a road.

★ Can you recognise a hole?

Only 44% of the people interviewed recognised that this drawing represents a hole. Not a single person who hadn't had a school education recognised it!

★ A cupboard, a church or a school?

86% of the town people recognised this drawing as a cupboard. But in the country only 14% people gave the correct answer. The drawing was named as a church or a school. Some people only saw doors.

Was it difficult for you to read any of the pictures? The country people may never have seen a cupboard like the one in the drawing. And perhaps you are not familiar with the hoe? Did you have a problem for this reason? The survey shows that we have to learn to 'read' pictures just as we have to learn to read words.

One thing at a time

★ Look at an object in front of you, perhaps a book or a pen or some paper. Look at the object for a few seconds. Are there any colours in the object?
Look again. Is the object worn or damaged in any way?
Look again. Is there any light reflected on it?

When you looked at the colour you didn't think about any worn or damaged parts. You chose what you wanted to see. Or rather, you chose what you wanted to think about from what you saw.

Your eye can't see everything. It

records only a very small part of the complicated world in front of it. Then your mind thinks about a very small amount of the information your eye is recording.

I have told you what to look at. Usually you *choose* what to look at. You choose what interests you at the moment. If you are hungry you will only look for a café or restaurant. If you are interested in architecture you will see the shapes of windows or roof decoration when someone else in the same street will see Volvos and Mercedes.

Our feelings affect how we see: if we are happy or sad we will see different things or we may see the same things but in a different way.

What about you?

★★ If you are with some friends at the moment ask them what they notice about the place you are in. Or choose a time when you have all been together and ask them to tell you what they remember seeing. (Perhaps going into a class together in the morning.)

The artist also sees what interests him or her. Monet was interested in light and colour and so that is what he painted. Canaletto was interested in architectural detail.

Claude Monet (1840–1926) 'The Thames Below Westminster' (National Gallery, London) Monet was one of the French Impressionist painters. He loved light and colour. He visited London twice and painted this picture of the Houses of Parliament in 1900. Note how the dark tone of the sky makes the water seem light.

Monet wanted a strong two dimensional design for his picture: note how he divided the picture up by the line of the bridge and Westminster and by the roadway on the right. The division of about two thirds for the sky, the use of horizontal shapes and the quiet tones give the picture a very still feeling.

Antonio Canaletto (1697–1768) 'The Doge's
Palace and Riva degli Schiavoni' (Wallace
Collection, London)
*Canaletto was interested in the details of
buildings and of people in their boats. He was
much more interested in three dimensional*
space than Monet: look at his strong use of
perspective (see also page 33). Note also how
Canaletto made use of tone: he painted the sky
dark above the front corner of the main
building, which made it seem light and come
forwards.

If you are a painter you know you have
to select. You can't paint everything, so
you select what interests you, and you
concentrate on making a good painting
of that. Here are some of the many
comments which artists have made in
the past about the need to select.

DRAWING IS SKILFUL CHOICE.

MICHELANGELO
(1475-1564)

BEGINNERS WANT TO SHOW EVERYTHING.

DELACROIX (1798-1863)

ART IS NOT A COPY OF NATURE
BUT A NEW OBJECT IN ITS
OWN RIGHT... IN THIS SENSE
IT IS A PART OF NATURE
LIKE ANY OTHER OBJECT.

ANDRÉ GIDE (1869-1951)

EVERY PORTRAIT THAT IS PAINTED WITH FEELING IS A PORTRAIT OF THE ARTIST NOT OF THE SITTER.

IT DEPENDS LITTLE ON THE OBJECT, MUCH ON THE MOOD IN ART.

OSCAR WILDE (1854-1900)

EMERSON (1803-1882)

So a painting shows us the painter's character, interests and feelings as much as the objects he has painted.

Many artists say that nature is

chaotic and a complete mess! They say that art must be organised and then people can understand it.

NATURE IS USUALLY WRONG!

JAMES MCNEIL WHISTLER (1834-1903)

LIFE IS VERY NICE, BUT IT LACKS FORM. IT'S THE AIM OF ART TO GIVE IT SOME.

JEAN ANOUILH (b. 1910)

ART IS A LIE THAT MAKES US REALISE THE TRUTH.

PABLO PICASSO (1881-1973)

Artists choose what to think about and choose what to paint. They also emphasise, even exaggerate in order to

make their point. (Doesn't everyone do this?)

THE WORK OF ART IS THE EXAGGERATION OF AN IDEA.

ANDRÉ GIDE (1869-1951)

★ If Monet was interested in light and colour and Canaletto in detail, what do you think the following artists were interested in:
Turner page 16, de Hooch page 23, van der Weyden page 25, Uccello page 34, Hobbema page 36, the artist from Basholi page 38.
These are the ideas I used in my answers. They might help you. (If you want to compare your answers with mine, see page 83.)
– space and the character of trees
– dignity, beauty, quietness
– drama of light and colour
– telling a story and rich patterns
– expensive quality of houses, furniture and clothes
– complicated patterns of shapes

I thought she was real

When I last went to Madame Tussaud's Wax Museum in London I wanted to buy some postcards. I chose several cards and took them to the assistant who was standing behind the counter and held them out to her. I waited, but she remained bent over her work. Suddenly I realised that she was a wax figure as well! I thought she was real!

Yes, art can deceive and make us think that it is real life. But it doesn't do it by imitating everything about real life: it can't do that. We supply the sense of reality. In this case, I expected to see an assistant behind the counter. I only thought of the assistant as someone who would take my cards and ask for the money. I was thinking about other things as well (where I would go next, whether I was hungry or not, etc.), so when I saw an object which looked like an assistant I thought it was one.

So, in fact, I supplied the reality. The artist was clever to make the right shape and to dress the figure in the right sort of clothes.

The assistant is made of wax!

Here is a violin painted on the back of a door at Chatsworth House. We don't expect to see a painting there so we think, for a brief moment, that it is a real violin. Painters who do this are clever, as they produce a temporary illusion. But is an illusion so very important?

Jan van der Vaart (c. 1653–1727) 'Violin' (Chatsworth House, Derbyshire)
This picture is painted on the State Music Room door. It is intended to look as if it is a real violin and not a picture of one! (There is another illusion painting of fruit and vegetables in 'The Annunciation' by Crivelli on page 39.)

Plato thought that all artists want to create illusions; and he didn't approve of illusions! He said that 'lovers of truth' should prefer carpenters to artists, because carpenters make real objects and artists only make illusions. We know now that the sculptors and probably the painters of Plato's Greece weren't just imitating nature; they were selecting, emphasising and creating new objects.

And indeed, many of the great artists of modern times have claimed the same for their own art. Note the ideas of Klee, Munch and Magritte in this book.

> I DECIDED TO STOP TRYING TO PAINT ILLUSIONS. IT DIDN'T INTEREST ME TO COPY AN OBJECT. WHY SHOULD I PAINT THE OUTSIDE OF AN APPLE? WHAT INTEREST CAN THERE BE IN COPYING AN OBJECT WHICH NATURE PROVIDES IN UNLIMITED QUANTITIES? WHAT IS IMPORTANT IS WHAT THE ARTIST FEELS ABOUT AN OBJECT, AND HOW HE IS ABLE TO CONTROL AND TO ORGANISE HIS SENSATIONS AND EMOTIONS.

HENRI MATISSE (1869 - 1954)

How to understand the language of paintings

Paint is your partner

You select what you see according to your interests: you can't see and think about everything at once. And, of course, the artist is the same. Paintings represent what the artist thinks is important.

The artist has an individual character but so does the paint! The character of the paint determines what the artist paints and how he or she paints.

Look at these two details of paintings. The one on the left is a fresco painting and the one on the right is an oil painting. The character of fresco painting gives rather flat, simple colours. The character of oil painting gives immense richness of colour and fine changes of light and dark.

Fresco painting and oil painting

Most artists used fresco painting on walls (or egg tempera on panels) until the 15th century. They painted their colours onto wet plaster . . . directly onto the wall. It was very difficult to show detail and to represent different qualities of material and texture.

Oil painting was invented in about 1400. The van Eyck painting of *The Arnolfini Marriage* is one of the very first oil paintings. Oil paint has different characteristics from paint used in frescoes. It dries slowly and the artist can paint on top of paint. Van Eyck was a master of texture. He could show qualities of velvet, lace, gold and skin.

Giotto di Bondone (c. 1266–1337) Detail of 'The Lamentation' (The Arena Chapel, Padua) See page 56 for the complete picture.

Jan van Eyck (1390–1441) Detail of 'The Arnolfini Marriage' (National Gallery, London) See page 65 for the complete picture.

FRESCO
Plaster dries in one day. The paint must mix with fresh plaster. So each day Giotto put on a small area of plaster and painted on to it. He took nine days to paint this picture. He began with the angels at the top. (Day 1)

GIOTTO DI BONDONE   BIRTH OF JESUS   FRESCO

Here are some tubes of modern oil paint. Oil paint can be thick or thin; smooth or rough. The colours may be burning hot or ice cold; they may have the richness of a king's cloak or the mud of a country lane; they may reflect the warm, bright light of a summer's day or the cold of a dark winter's evening.

WASH: THE ARTIST PAINTS WIDE AREAS OF THIN COLOUR OVER THE PAPER OR CANVAS
GLAZE: THIN COLOUR OVER OPAQUE COLOUR.

IMPASTO: THIS IS AN ITALIAN WORD. IT IS USED TO MEAN THICK PAINT.

SCUMBLING:
THE ARTIST DRAGS THICK PAINT ACROSS OTHER AREAS OF PAINT. THE COLOURS UNDERNEATH CAN BE SEEN. THESE COLOURS MIGHT BE COOL COLOURS CONTRASTING RICHLY WITH THE WARM COLOURS ON TOP.

15

Joseph Mallord William Turner (1775–1851)
'The Fighting Temeraire' (National Gallery,
London)
Turner was probably the greatest British painter
of all time. He left 500 oil paintings and over
20,000 watercolours to the nation. His paintings
are mainly landscapes and seascapes.

The Temeraire was a warship and fought at
the Battle of Trafalgar in 1805. In 1838 she was
out of date. She was taken into the River
Thames by a steam tug boat and she was broken
up. Many people thought that this symbolised
the end of the British navy (the sunset represents
the end of the day and of the British navy!).

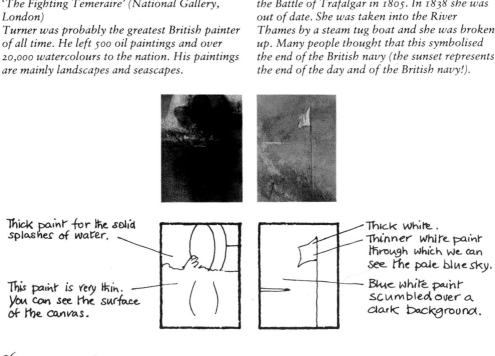

Thick paint for the solid splashes of water.

This paint is very thin. You can see the surface of the canvas.

Thick white.
Thinner white paint through which we can see the pale blue sky.

Blue white paint scumbled over a dark background.

Turner understood the qualities of paint. He painted large thin washes when he started his painting. Then he painted with thick colours, sometimes using a brush and sometimes a knife. Sometimes he scumbled the paint; through the holes and gaps we can see the paint beneath. This gives richness and depth to the picture.

Turner used thin paint in the shadows and thick paint on the solid objects in the light.

★ If you look at some shadows near you now you may feel that you can't touch them. Objects in shadow are mysterious and untouchable. Now look at an object or part of an object in the light. Doesn't it seem more solid?

Have a look at Rembrandt's *Titus* on page 43 and Bacon's *Triptych 1971* on page 74 for the use of paint in this way.

What can different pens and pencils do?

Paint is the artist's partner. You can only do what your partner can do and enjoys doing.

★ Try a simple experiment: find as many different pens and pencils as you can. See what sort of marks each pen or pencil 'enjoys' making.

Here are some that I have tried:

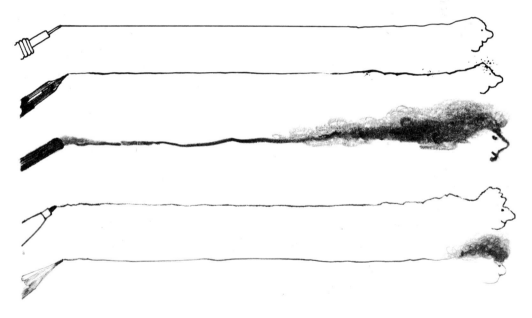

The first line was done with a pen used by engineers, architects and graphic designers. The line doesn't change in thickness. This type of pen is not intended to express feelings. The artist can use such a pen but only for fine detail and for precision. This sort of pen can't show large areas of shadow or exciting, strong lines which can show the movement of an animal, for example.

The second line was done with an ordinary, old-fashioned school pen. The nib is metal and it bends and opens, so the line can vary in thickness. This variation of line can show movement and excitement. Sometimes, as it digs into the paper, it splutters and makes a blob or scatters spots of ink everywhere. Some artists use even this quality! If you wanted a straight line of even thickness you would never use such a pen.

The third line was made by a piece of charcoal. Charcoal is very soft and it is easy to show areas of shadow. This is the only one of the five examples which produces large areas of shadow naturally and 'happily'. If the artist wants to show a lot of shadow then he or she would choose charcoal rather than any of the pens above.

The fourth line was made by a felt tip pen. There are many types of felt tip pen: this pen has a soft quality. You can see how it has dragged over the roughness of the paper. The broken parts of the line suggest light and gentleness.

The fifth line was made by a pencil. It is hard enough to make a fine and delicate line and soft enough to make a rich dark shadow.

Paint (or in the above examples, pens and pencils) is the artist's partner. A good painter makes the paint look fresh and happy! A good painting shows the character of the artist *and* the paint as well as the object represented.

Reproductions of paintings

All the paintings in this book are reproductions. Good reproductions can represent the qualities of thick and thin paint and smooth and rough surfaces. However, although the quality is represented it is still not the 'real thing'. If you touch the picture you will feel smooth paper. And you will not see the light crossing the surface and passing through the different layers of colour. Some reproductions are printed on paper which isn't smooth and feels like canvas; this is even more disappointing because when you realise that it is false you feel deceived! People who like looking at paintings very often become tired of reproductions, however good they are.

Shape

The living shape

★ Which sentence describes which picture, do you think?

In picture . . . the forces push outwards.

In picture . . . there is a struggle between the forces pushing inwards and the forces pushing outwards. In picture . . . the forces push inwards.

Rudolph Arnheim, the psychologist, believes that every shape has character and that there is a feeling of tension, relaxation, push and pull within and around every shape. His analysis of the shapes is on page 83.

★ Do you agree with Arnheim? If you agree with him then this might demonstrate that we respond to shapes in similar ways.

Shapes people like

Barnhart, a psychologist, showed these shapes to 50 university students. (The shapes were cut out of blue paper and placed on white card.) The students were asked to arrange the shapes in the order they liked.

★ Before you read what the students thought, answer these questions:
Which two shapes do you prefer the most?
Which two shapes do you like the least?
Why do you like or dislike those shapes?

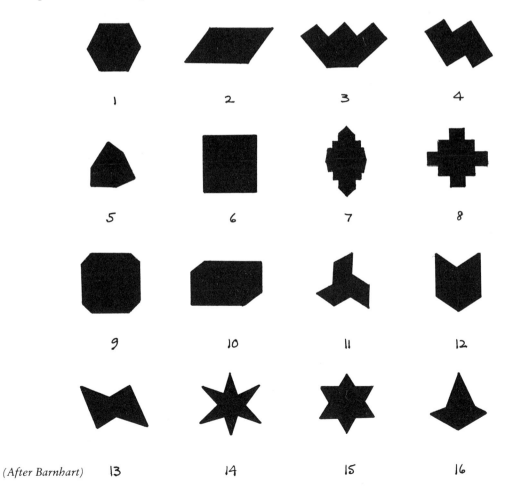

(After Barnhart) 13

The most popular shapes of the 50 students were 7 and 14.
The least popular shapes of the 50 students were 5 and 11.

There were three types of reason given by the students. These were:
1 Reasons based on the abstract character of the shape; symmetry, balance, complexity, etc.
2 Association with nice or with unpleasant experiences.
3 The possibility of using the shape in a design.
90% of the students gave the first type of reason. Very few gave the third type of reason. What did you think?

In another experiment, a psychologist called McElroy, showed some shapes to 380 boys and 399 girls aged between 9 and 16 in three Scottish schools. Most of the boys preferred rounded and curved shapes. The majority of the girls preferred angular shapes like triangles!

Is this research useful? Does it help us to appreciate pictures? What do you think? I think it does . . . a little bit! Such research shows that people can share common feelings about shape and reminds one that painting is language.

The golden rectangle

★ Which of these rectangles do you prefer?
★★ Show the rectangles to ten of your friends and note down which one they prefer.

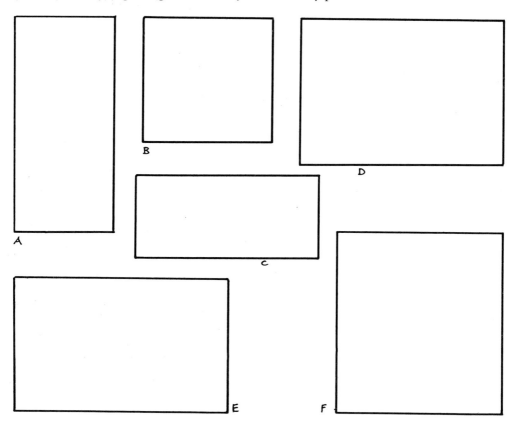

The majority seem to prefer Rectangle E. Did you find that? Rectangle E is a golden rectangle! The golden proportions are . . . 5:8! The classical artists of Greece loved this proportion. The shape gave them the feeling of balance and eternal life. But a lot of artists don't like the golden proportion. They feel it is too calm!

For those of you who like mathematics, here is the mathematical basis for the golden proportion.

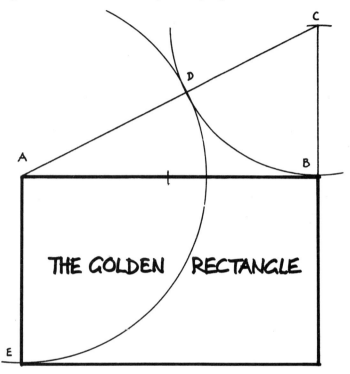

THE GOLDEN / RECTANGLE

Which is the friendly house?

★★ Ask as many people as you can and see what they say. I think they will say that the house on the right is the friendly house.

We have looked at faces since we were babies. What do you think these two are thinking?

In the face on the right the eyebrows are straight, horizontal, close together and close to the eyes. If the eyebrows are dark it emphasises the expression of anger. The mouth is short and turned down . . . it is rather grim. In the face on the left the eyebrows are lifted away from the eyes. They are rounded and light.

Don't you agree that the face on the left looks friendly and the one on the right looks unfriendly?

Psychologists believe that most people think that the house on the right looks friendly because it reminds them of a friendly face. They call this 'physiognomic perception'!

★ We often respond to objects as if they were people. Which of the words below would you use to describe these trees?

graceful   dignified   calm   excited dreamy   ugly   strong   frightening

★ If you would like to experiment, see if you can find objects around you which you could describe with any of these words.

★★ Here are four pictures. Which of the words opposite would you use to describe them? Compare your answers with your friends. Do your chosen words agree?

Jean-Honoré Fragonard (1732–1806) 'The Swing' (Wallace Collection, London)
Fragonard has only included a few centimetres of vertical and horizontal line in his picture! (Compare with the picture by de Hooch.) He wanted to express the carefree character of life in the French royal court . . . and vertical and horizontal lines express quietness and dignity!

Pieter de Hooch (1629–1684) 'A Boy Bringing Pomegranates' (Wallace Collection, London)
During the 17th century the Netherlands became a rich country. This painting shows a merchant's house. The boy is bringing fruit imported from the Mediterranean. Notice the strong perspective lines on the floor. (Compare with the picture on page 39.) But also notice that there are strong vertical and horizontal lines and shapes which give a calm and dignified feeling to the picture. Three centuries later these rectangular shapes were used again by the modern artist from the Netherlands, Mondrian.

〉〉〉→

Edvard Munch (1863–1944) 'The Scream' (National Gallery, Oslo)
Munch lived and worked with the Impressionists in France for a short time. He later returned home to Norway where he became increasingly sad and lonely. This famous painting of 'The Scream' expresses fear, horror and conflict.
Content: We see a thin, frightened person with mouth open, bulging eyes and raised hand. We also see two threatening, dark figures.
Form: The strong perspective lines give depth and space but all the other lines emphasise the flatness of the picture, so there is a conflict between the depth and the flatness. Furthermore, there is a conflict between the straight lines of the path and the curving, swirling lines of the sky and sea. These conflicts in the form (lines and shapes) express the conflict in the painter's mind. Munch once said, 'A work of art can only come from inside a person.'

Willem van de Velde (The Younger) (1633–1707) 'Ships in a Calm' (Wallace Collection, London)
In 18th century Holland ships were very important. Holland was a rich trading nation and the merchants wanted to possess pictures of the ships which brought them their wealth. Van de Velde was one of the many painters of the sea and of ships who lived and worked in Holland at this time. In this picture he has chosen to paint ships in a calm. No wind, no sailing, no trade! Not such a happy picture, perhaps, for a merchant! The gentle differences between the tones of sky, sea and sail, the vertical lines of the masts and the drooping curves of the sails all express calmness and peace.

Rogier van der Weyden (1399–1464) 'Portrait of a Lady' (National Gallery, London)
Rogier van der Weyden and Jan van Eyck were the two greatest painters of Northern Europe in the 15th century. They both lived in what we now call Belgium. They were both 'naturalistic' painters and they gave individual character to the people they painted.

In this picture van der Weyden expresses the quiet dignity of this woman. The composition (see pages 53–59) is strong; the triangle of white headdress fills the top part of the picture. And the pale tone (see pages 45-49) glows with light because all the other tones are darker. These tones are calmly organised (there are no other bright areas of tone). Contrast the lively and excited scattering of light tones in Hilliard's painting of a young man on page 61.

Shapes show thoughts . . . even woolly thoughts!

My copy of Rogier van der Weyden's *Portrait of a Lady*, is easily recognisable. For that purpose my drawing is quite good! But usually we want a drawing to be more than merely recognisable. We want it to have artistic character.

Look at the nose I have drawn and compare it to the nose in the painting. The line I have used is just a general curve: there is no particular character of shape and line in it. Look at all the other general shapes I have drawn and compare them with those in the painting.

One of the chief differences between great art and very ordinary art is this difference between the general and the particular. Generalised, 'woolly' shapes and lines show generalised and 'woolly' thinking!

An artist's shapes

★ Look through all the paintings in this book, and try to find the details below. I have chosen details of shapes which I feel are typical of the artists and their styles.

25

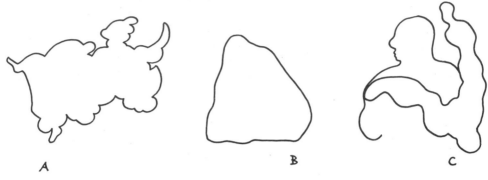

A   B   C

How easily can you see and recognise shape in pictures?

The shapes an artist uses often show his character and even the character of his period.
Detail A: The flowing, tight, quick curves are typical of Fragonard and of many artists of 18th century France (see page 23).
Detail B: The simplicity of this shape is typical of Giotto (see page 56).
Detail C: This is a desperate shape. It twists with tension. It is a typical shape of Francis Bacon's paintings (see page 74).

The shape belongs to the object and to the artist

The shape you draw or paint must express what you feel about an object as well as look like it. Here are some of the things that I think artists have felt about the faces they have painted.
★ Which paintings in the book do you think I am referring to? (See my answers on page 83.)
1 One artist uses the pattern of the face as a decoration.

2 Another artist wants us to appreciate the beautiful curving lines of the eyes, the nose, mouth and neck.
3 Another feels passionate about life. He wants to show us excitement, passion, even danger and a feeling of violence.
4 Another thinks that the face is eternal. He doesn't want to show individual differences.
5 Another loves the individual's face. He feels that it represents all of us. It represents all our hopes and happinesses, all our fates and sufferings.
6 Another hears the cry of pain and fear. He sees the end of each person's world. He looks beyond the face into the infinite blackness.

In conclusion, it is easy to draw the shape of something so that other people can recognise it. But that ability is not enough to satisfy us. We want to understand what the artist felt and thought when he painted the picture. These feelings and ideas are communicated to us by his particular, personal use of shape.

Lines people like

The psychologist Lundholm asked eight people to draw ugly lines and beautiful lines. He studied the lines and then concluded that beautiful lines are gentle and continuous and the curves are repeated. Ugly lines are discontinuous and irregular; there are sharp angles in them and they change direction.

★★ Ask your friends to draw what they think are ugly and beautiful lines. Study them and find out whether the lines have anything in common. Do you think Lundholm was right?

In another experiment, two psychologists, Poffenberger and Barrows, showed 18 lines to 500 people and gave them a list of adjectives.

★ Here are the 18 lines. How would you describe lines A, C, H and J? Use these adjectives.

sad   happy   furious   lazy   hard
powerful   agitated   weak
severe   gentle   quiet

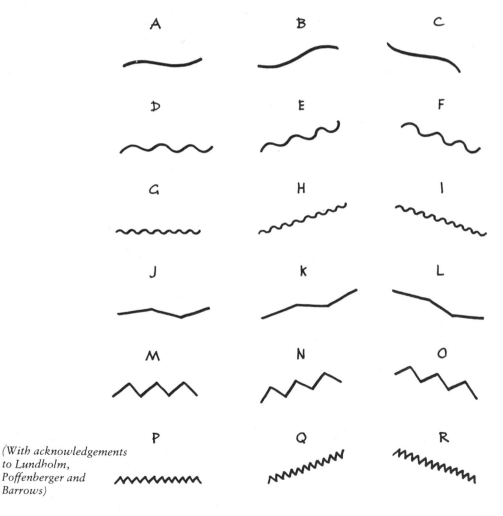

(With acknowledgements to Lundholm, Poffenberger and Barrows)

I showed lines A, C, H and J to a group of 70 people. They described them as follows:

A (curving)   sad (29), quiet (18), lazy (9), happy (8), weak (5), others (1)

C (downward curving)   sad (24), gentle (19), weak (8), quiet (8), lazy (6), others (5)

H (rising)   happy (35), agitated (20), gentle (11), others (4)

J (angular)   hard (24), powerful (23), furious (7), agitated (6), severe (5), others (5)

★★ Show the lines to as many people as you can and ask them to choose an adjective for each line. See how the answers compare with the figures above.

Many people interpret the character of lines in a similar way so, once again, this shows that painting is a language.

Here are two drawings by Klee. He has used angular lines in one of them and curving lines in the other. These lines affect the way we feel about the subjects he has drawn.

Paul Klee (1879–1940) 'Low Tide' (Paul Klee Foundation, Berne)
Paul Klee was like William Hogarth (see page 3) in that they both wanted to find a 'grammar of art' and they both enjoyed humour. But whereas the humour of Hogarth was 'of the Earth', the humour of Klee was 'of the Heavens'. Klee said his grammar was based on dot, line, plane and space. He called these 'elements' and said they must be found in every picture.

The character of the material, in this case pen and ink on paper, and the 'elements' of line, dot, plane and space express the feeling of the artist. In this drawing, Klee expresses his feelings about the beach, rocks, pools and seaweed when the tide is low. And perhaps this also represents for him the quiet, deep stirrings of his own mind. How would you interpret 'Storm Spirit'?

Paul Klee was born near Berne in Switzerland. He studied in Germany and lived there until 1933. He left Germany and returned to Switzerland when the Nazis made life and freedom difficult.

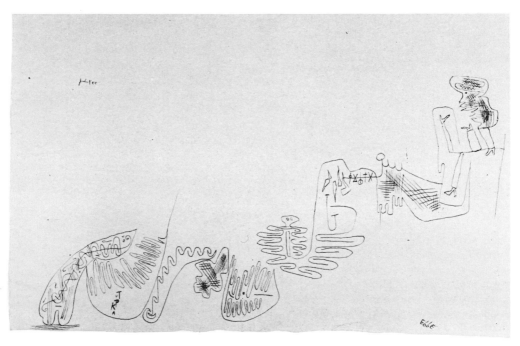

Paul Klee (1879–1940) 'Storm Spirit' (Paul Klee Foundation, Berne)

Taking a line for a walk

Paul Klee was an artist and a teacher. He believed that lines, dots and textures have life. One day he told the story below to his students and drew a 'line story' on the blackboard.

★ Read the story, then use a pen or a pencil to draw a line which expresses each part of the story. Show your drawing to a friend and see if he or she can guess Paul Klee's story called 'Taking a Line for a Walk'.

The line is born. It begins to move. After a moment it stops. It wants to breathe. Then it looks backwards to see how far we have come. It is not sure which way to go: it starts several paths but returns. There is a river in front of us. We must cross it. So we take a boat; there is a bridge further up the river. We go across a ploughed field, and then through a thick forest . . . we meet some basket makers on their way home, they are in a cart. They have a child with

funny, curly hair. Later the air becomes hot and damp; the night falls. There is a flash of lightning on the horizon, though the stars are still twinkling overhead.

How full of events our little journey is! The first part was happy, then came the difficulties; we were very nervous. We were frightened. Before the storm a swarm of flies came at us. Anger and killing! Our good purpose is our guide, even in the woods and the darkness. The flash of lightning reminds us of the fever chart of a sick child.

Paul Klee loved the character of line. You might think that he just invented the idea of the line for this story. In fact he got the idea from his everyday life. His little son, Felix, was very ill a few months before he wrote the story and he drew Felix's fever chart in his diary every day. An artist like Klee recognises the character of line in everyday life, and he uses this knowledge in his pictures.

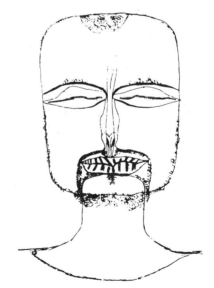

Paul Klee (1879–1940) 'Lost in Thought (Self-Portrait)'
You might like to compare the way in which Paul Klee has used a pen with the section on pens and pencils on page 17.

29

More walking lines

A man is walking along a path through the fields. His dog is running around him but is never far away.

★ Can you tell a story about the lines below?

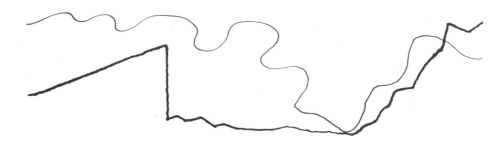

Space and volume

The grammar of depth

These are some of the ways in which artists show depth in their pictures.

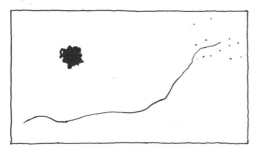

As soon as you put a mark on a piece of paper you can imagine the space around it and beyond it. The rectangle is like a frame: we want to look through it.

Warm colours (red, yellow, orange) seem to come forward, and cool colours (blue, purple) seem to be in the distance. (Paul Cézanne used warm and cool colours to make volume and space, see page 40. Also see how Turner used cool colours to show distance, on page 16.)

Strong, dark tones seem to come forward and pale tones seem to be more distant. And a strong colour seems to be nearer than a paler colour. (See how Monet used dark tones, page 8.)

Thick paint seems to be nearer than thin paint. (See Turner's picture on page 16.)

Sharp detail seems to be nearer than vague, suggested shapes.

The darker side of an object seems to be nearer to us.

Shadows suggest volume. And volume suggests that there must be space around the object. (Many pictures use this technique. See the violin at Chatsworth on page 12, van Eyck's picture on page 65, and Rembrandt's picture on page 43.)

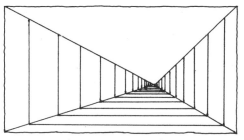

Perspective suggests space. It is the strongest technique the artist has for giving a feeling of depth to his pictures. (Note how the clouds in the sky of Turner's picture on page 16 get smaller and closer together as they go into the distance.)

Robert de Lisle (1288–1344) 'Crucifixion'
(British Museum, London)
This painting is flat; the artist has chosen a flat
pattern for the background instead of a
landscape. Each part of the pattern is repeated
indefinitely and this expresses the belief that the
subject of the picture will go on for ever. The
figure of Jesus Christ is not painted in quite the
same way as the other two figures. Christ is
painted rather flatly with strong, decorative
lines (particularly note Christ's clothes and the
ribs). The figures on either side are not so flat.
The artist has made the clothes look more real,
more three dimensional. The faces of these two
people are also slightly more naturalistic.
Perhaps the artist wanted to make these two
people a little more like individuals so that we
can put ourselves into the picture through them?

Pictures with and without perspective

The medieval artists didn't know about perspective; they didn't want to show depth in their pictures. They didn't want to make their people look like real, individual people in a real, individual scene. They wanted to show eternal timeless truth, the eternal timeless quality of their religious stories. So these artists didn't need to know about perspective! (See St John on page 61.)

In the European Renaissance period (from the 14th to 16th centuries), artists wanted to show the importance of the individual person and his or her possessions and surroundings. A flat medieval style couldn't show this level of reality and the artists needed a new technique. It was the Italian artist Brunelleschi who discovered the technique of perspective drawing. (See Crivelli's picture on page 39.)

Perspective

FILIPPO BRUNELLESCHI
1377 - 1446
ARCHITECT
PAINTER
SCULPTOR
AND INVENTOR
OF THE
REPRESENTATION
OF PERSPECTIVE

At first the artists of the Renaissance only had single-point perspective. Later they realised that they could have two-point perspective and still later multi-point perspective.

With two-point perspective they could turn an object (like a building) at an angle to the picture and draw two sides of it.

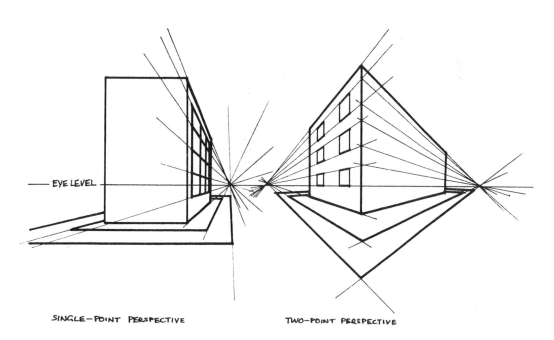

EYE LEVEL

SINGLE—POINT PERSPECTIVE

TWO—POINT PERSPECTIVE

Paolo Uccello worked all night on perspective exercises. When he went to bed at last, his wife complained. All he could say was, 'How delightful perspective is!' Although Uccello loved perspective he didn't fully understand it. He could apply the rules to buildings but he didn't know how to apply them to people. Look at this detail of a fallen soldier from the painting above.

Paolo Uccello (1397–1475) 'The Battle of San Romano' (National Gallery, London)
The strength of this picture is in the pattern of shapes of the horses, the weapons and the fields. Unfortunately, Uccello thought too much about perspective! It had just been discovered and it was a new fashion. Uccello spoiled his picture with it. Look at the weapons on the ground; they have been carefully arranged to show that Uccello understood the new principles of perspective.

Paolo Uccello (1397–1475) Detail of 'The Battle of San Romano' (National Gallery, London)
Did Uccello fully understand the principles of perspective? No! He could arrange the weapons correctly but he didn't understand that objects must get smaller as they go into the distance. The fallen soldier does not . . . his body is far too big (or his feet and legs are too small!).

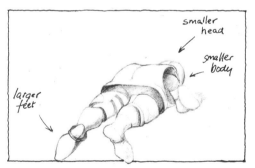

Sometimes an artist may not want to show things getting smaller as they go away from us. However, in this case, I think it was that Uccello didn't know how to do it. A language must be learnt. The technique of perspective which seems so natural to us now is an invented technique . . . part of the 'grammar of painting'.

Imagine you are standing in an absolutely flat desert. The far edge of the desert which you can see is your 'eye level'. If you crouch down your eye level, of course, lowers.

If you stand in the middle of a long, straight street (possibly a foolish thing to do!) the far end of the street will be on your eye level. The two sides of the road seem to come together on your eye level. And indeed most of the lines seem to come down to your eye level: the tops of the buildings, the tops and bottoms of windows, etc.

Wherever you are now you can probably see an example of these 'perspective lines' coming down to your eye level. Of course, some lines may be coming up to your eye level.

★ Look at the two sides of a table and see how they seem to get nearer together as they go away from you. If you continued these two lines they would meet on your eye level. Raise and lower your head as you look at the table and you will see the two lines of the sides of the table appearing to narrow as you lower your head, and widen as you raise your head.

As Uccello found out, perspective is not as easy as that! Like all bits of grammar there are exceptions! Only vertical and horizontal surfaces seem to meet on eye

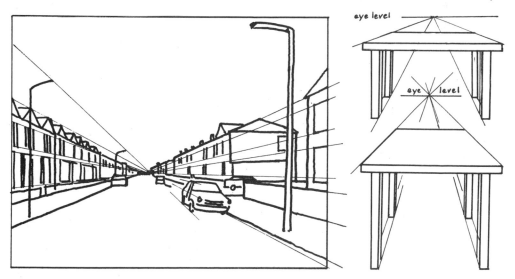

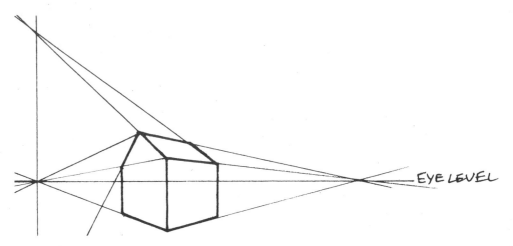

EYE LEVEL

level. Sloping roof tops, for example, don't meet on eye level!

For 500 years, artists in Europe made use of perspective drawing in their pictures. During this century, however, many artists have decided they don't want to paint pictures with perspective in them.

Meyndert Hobbema (1638–1709) 'The Avenue, Middelharnis' (National Gallery, London) Hobbema used a single-point perspective 250 years after it was discovered. However, although the painting has great depth it is also strong as a pattern of shapes across the picture.

Can you read depth?

★ Study these plans and texts and decide which go together. Then decide which picture in the book they describe. (Remember that a plan is a 'bird's eye view'. We are looking down!)

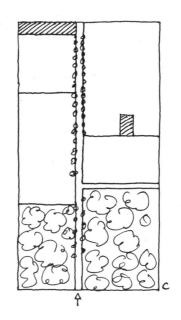

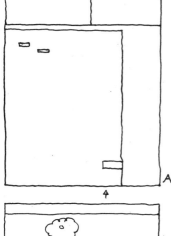

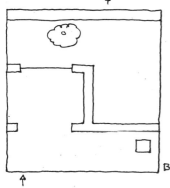

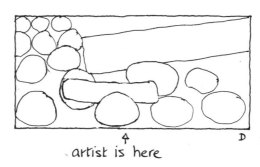

artist is here

1 We are standing in the middle of the road. Another road joins it on the right, after about 100 metres. Beyond this road, on the right, there is a farm and in the distance, to the left of the road, there is a village with a church.

2 We are on the edge of a crowd of people who are standing and kneeling close together. They are in front of a long rock. There seems to be no distance behind the rock.

3 On the right hand side of the picture there is a road or a promenade. This runs alongside a river. In the distance, on the right of the picture, are some tall buildings. On the left of the picture there are a few boats in front of a bridge.

4 We are inside a house. We are looking across a room and through an open doorway into a hallway. On the far side of the hallway there is an open door. Through the door we can see a tree in a yard. On the other side of the yard there is another building.

(See the answers on page 83.)

Into the picture or across the picture . . . or both?

In this 17th century Punjabi picture there are no perspective lines. The artist has designed a 'flat' picture. We see the carpet as a rectangle from above, and we only see one side of the house. We see the pond from above but the people and the tree from the side. But we do see space; we do think that the boy is on the other side of the pond and not on top of a squashed circle! Couldn't this artist draw perspective like Western Renaissance artists? He didn't need to! He could tell the story clearly in his own style and produce beautiful shapes and colours.

Crivelli wanted to show depth in his picture and he used a simple single-point perspective. However the arrangement of the shapes in his picture is still very strong across the picture.

A painter from Basholi in the Punjab (c. 1665) 'Resourceful Radha' (Victoria and Albert Museum, London)
This picture is about a perfect lover. The lover (the lady) sees a servant who is going to cut down the tree. The lady used to meet the God Krishna under the tree. So she takes the axe and throws it into the pond! Krishna is in the house.

right
Carlo Crivelli (1430–1495) 'The Annunciation' (National Gallery, London)
Although Crivelli represented space by using strong perspective lines he also made a strong pattern of shapes across the picture. Notice how he painted the people and the details on the buildings in the distance as carefully as the people and details near to us at the front of the picture. This makes the distant objects come forward and flattens the shapes. Note the illusion of the fruit and vegetables at the bottom of the picture.

Paul Cézanne (1839–1906) 'The
Gardener Vallier' (Tate Gallery,
London)
Cézanne wanted to show volume
and space. He said that the
underlying shapes in nature are the
sphere, the cylinder and the cone.
Although he was interested in space
in his pictures he wanted to give a
solid strength across his pictures.
The strong design of dark and light
tones look very much like Picasso's
'cubist' picture opposite. This was one
of Cézanne's last pictures (1906).
Many people regard Cézanne as one
of the greatest painters of the last
100 years and the inventor of
'cubism'.

Vincent van Gogh (1853–1890)
'Flowering Plum Tree' (National
Museum Vincent van Gogh,
Amsterdam)
Van Gogh wanted to find a
language of painting which he
could use to express his emotions.
He learned from the
Impressionists but he also learned
from the Japanese artists. He
learned from the Japanese how to
organise flat shapes across his
pictures.
  He was a lonely and often
desperate man. In a time of great
personal trouble he cut off his ear
and sent it to a friend. Finally, he
shot himself.

Pablo Picasso (1881–1973) 'Seated Nude' (Tate Gallery, London)
Picasso painted this picture three years after Cézanne painted his gardener. It seems a natural development from one to the other. Cézanne's picture is both a portrait of an individual man and a strongly designed picture. However, Picasso's picture is really just a picture! Picasso has concentrated on designing a solid effect in which the person and the background are both solid and similar in colour. This is called a 'cubist' painting because the objects are shown with flat sides and look very solid.

Cézanne always talked about space and volume. And he did give a feeling of space in his pictures. However, he didn't want a deep depth; he wanted all the objects to be solid and designed strongly across the surface of the picture.

Van Gogh, like some of the other painters of the Impressionist period, was interested in Japanese prints. And Japanese artists until this century were always very strong designers of 'flat' pictures.

Picasso certainly made pictures which have volume and depth. However, he wanted to keep our eyes on the surface and to remind us that his paintings are paintings and not illusions.

In conclusion, it is technically easy to give an illusion of depth. However, I believe that a strong two dimensional design is just as important as a feeling of depth . . . perhaps more important. All great paintings seem to have this characteristic.

The grammar of volume

★ First of all, make a fist like this:

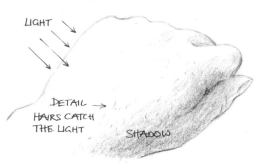

If possible hold your hand in a strong light. You will see the volume of your hand by the light and shade. One side catches the light and one side is turned away from the light. You will see the volume of each finger and each knuckle in the same way.

Can you see any little hairs on your hand which catch the light? They are probably on the edge of the shadows. They are catching the light and you see them brightly lit against the shadow.

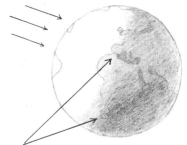

IN THIS AREA OF THE WORLD IT IS EVENING. THE SUN IS LOW IN THE SKY. THE TREES AND THE WALLS CATCH THE LIGHT.

When the sun is low in the sky it is crossing the surface of the earth and this makes the trees, houses, etc. very sharp and bright.

Rembrandt van Rijn (1606–1669) 'The Artist's Son Titus' (Wallace Collection, London)
Rembrandt was one of the greatest artists of all time. In spite of this he died a poor and sad man. People didn't understand the language of painting which he developed. They wanted to be able to recognise everything in the picture which they were paying for; and so people stopped paying him!

His favourite subject for his paintings was people. In the painting reproduced here he has shown us his son. The painting is in the typical style of Rembrandt: a dark background and the light coming strongly from one side. The face is half in shadow and half in light. In Rembrandt's pictures we have the mystery of human nature in the shadows and what we think we understand in the light.

There is a slight frown on the face of Titus, his eyes look slightly pained and there is a suggestion of a smile. In every painting by Rembrandt we have this warm understanding of human nature; when he was alive, people didn't want to pay for this human warmth.

detail and thick paint

Rembrandt put all the detail and colour and the thickness of paint on the change of the volume from light into darkness.

Cézanne thought colour was more important than shadow. He tried to show volume by variations of colour. On the change of the volume he placed his richest colour.

Paul Cézanne (1839–1906) 'Self-Portrait' (National Gallery, London)
Cézanne worked with the Impressionists but they were interested in light and colour and he was more interested in light and colour to make volumes and structures. In this self-portrait he has used small brush strokes of different colours to create the volume. Generally speaking, cool colours seem to recede and warm colours seem to come forwards.

For 1,000 years artists didn't want to paint volume (see the medieval illustrations on pages 32 and 61). Then Giotto, the first of the Renaissance artists, wanted to show the emotions of individual people, not symbols (see his painting on page 56). He needed volume to represent the difference between individual people.

Here are some simple ways of showing volume which you might like to copy:

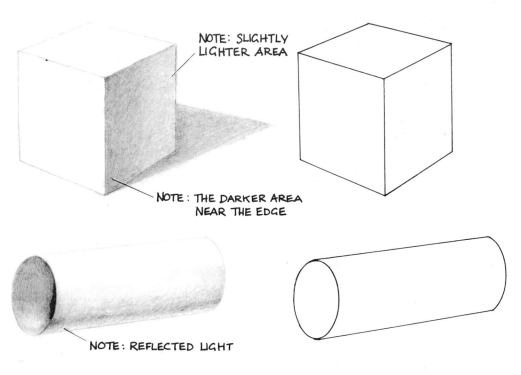

NOTE: SLIGHTLY LIGHTER AREA

NOTE: THE DARKER AREA NEAR THE EDGE

NOTE: REFLECTED LIGHT

HEAD LIGHTER THAN THE BACKGROUND

HEAD LIGHTER AND DARKER THAN THE BACKGROUND

Tone

Tone means the degree of darkness or lightness of a colour. A black and white photograph represents all the colours as tones. A good artist organises the tones to express an idea or a feeling in his picture. Let me give you some idea of what I mean.

In this picture there are several equally light areas and they are all about the same size. When your eye arrives at the picture it moves from one light area to another. Your eye is restless, your mind searches for order.

It is possible to use this restless movement deliberately. Look at the restless movement in the following pictures:
– Hilliard's picture on page 61. The patches of light are small and give a feeling of carefree enjoyment.
– Bacon's picture on page 74. There are three large, light areas at the sides of the picture: these pull the eyes from side to side. There is light at the side of the stairs and along the person's arms and these two shapes twist and turn. Tone is used in this picture to disturb us, as my plan on the right shows.

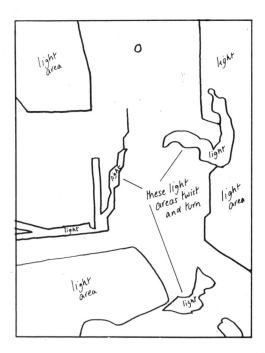

In this picture there is an order to the tones. The clouds are the lightest tone, then the pond, then the sky and the field, then the tree, then the hills and finally the hedge. The clouds seem to glow with light. The hills, fields and trees seem to be dark and calm and rich.

In this picture there is a different order of tones. Now the pond is the lightest and the field is the next lightest. Notice how the mood has changed. There is a feeling of threat or danger. Perhaps it is the threat of a storm and perhaps the picture expresses an emotional threat? (See also the picture on page 73 by Klee.) Of course, within each area there may be some smaller areas of different tone. Within the tree there may be darker shadows and on some leaves there may be light. But the main impression is of one area of tone.

The artist can lead our eyes by organising the tones. In this picture the repetition of the heads, their rhythmic placing and the repetition of light tones all lead our eyes along the faces to look at the main figure.

★ Here is a picture by Cotman. Can you find about eight different tones? (See my answer on page 83.) Notice how Cotman directs our eyes to the wall; he has put a very dark cow against it, and this attracts our eye.

John Sell Cotman (1782–1842) 'The Water Tower, York' (Whitworth Art Gallery, University of Manchester)
This is a watercolour painting. The English were particularly good at painting in watercolours. No white paint was used; white areas are shown by the use of the white paper. Cotman had a wonderful sense of tone and in this picture he makes us look most of all at the brightest part of the picture. He has put a dark cow here to provide a strong tonal contrast. Although the painting is small (only 22.2 × 43.2 cm) the shapes are so full of character that it could be a huge picture.

Francisco Goya (1746–1828) 'A Stormy Night' (British Museum, London)
This picture is an etching; it has been printed from a copper plate. Goya was official painter to the Spanish court, and he painted many wonderful and truthful portraits of the royal family. However, Goya was very upset by the cruelty of some people to other people. He made hundreds of etchings representing what he saw and expressing what he felt about it.

In this picture a young woman tries to hold down her skirts in a strong wind. In the darkness of the night various shapes threaten her. Is it a young man behind her? Or is it a devil with black wings? Goya can make us look into the shadows of our own minds and see things we prefer not to think about! See also page 74.

★ And here is a picture by Goya. Can you analyse the order of the main tonal areas? (See my answer on page 84.)

★ Here are two outline drawings of pictures reproduced in this book. Trace the drawings and then try out alternative tones on them.

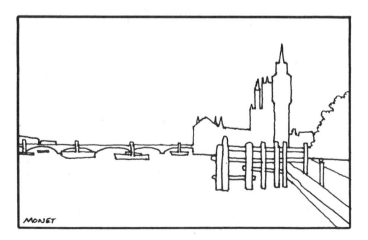

MONET

HOKUSAI

★ Here are four descriptions of the tones in four pictures in the book. If you can identify the pictures you have a good sense of tone! (Answers on page 84.)

1 In this picture the artist has put the lightest parts of the picture at the front: the first column on the left is the lightest part of all, the nearest corner of the building is light and the people in the boats at the front are lighter than those further away. The sky is just a little bit darker than the corner of the building and this makes it very bright.

2 The lightest part of the picture is the woman and so we look at her first. One of the ropes is very light and it leads our eye to her. The man's left arm is light and that also points to her. The heavy, dark tone of the tree is not very threatening because a 'stream' of light comes down from the left.

3 There is a slightly threatening feeling about this picture. The sky is darker than the wave which hangs huge and heavy above a mountain.

4 There is whiteness in the background and in the shapes; for example, the faces and the arms. Because there are a lot of light areas the eye continually moves around and the shapes and the lines encourage this movement.

Colour

Some ways of using colour

HELPING PEOPLE TO RECOGNISE THINGS

If artists want you to recognise objects in their pictures they will paint the objects in the colour you know. For example, an orange is just a round shape: we recognise it mainly by its colour. (See van Eyck's oranges on page 65.) In the picture by van der Vaart on page 12 the colour of the violin is the colour of a beautiful wood. He wanted people to think it was a real violin hanging on the door.

EXPRESSING FEELINGS

Some artists use colours to express their feelings. In the picture by Paul Klee on page 73 there is a lot of dark green and this makes the picture like a dream. On the other hand, Bacon, in his picture on page 74 has used a lot of black and white and these colours communicate violence.

DIRECTING ATTENTION

The artist can direct our attention to a part of the picture by the use of colour. For example, in the picture by Uccello on page 34, we look at the hero of the battle, Nicola da Tolentino, partly because he is riding a bright, white horse and is wearing a large red hat!

SYMBOLISING AN IDEA

To Christians in the middle ages in Europe, the colour blue meant faithfulness and the colour green meant hope, youth and joy. (Blue was also a very expensive colour and it was a sign of reverence to make the Virgin's dress blue.) There are a number of uses of symbolic colour in the painting by van Eyck on page 65. But many people today don't know what these colours

meant. Colour is a part of the language of painting: if you don't learn the language you won't understand it. When we look at a painting from the middle ages we don't understand much of what we see. (And we wouldn't understand most of the spoken language of the middle ages either!)

THOUSANDS OF COLOURS!

According to Jerome Bruner we can recognise more than seven million colours! Even in one day we may see many of these. Look around you at the moment and see how many red objects you can see: in my room I can see red book covers, red pens, red wallpaper and red paint. Each red is different; some reds are rather orange, some rather brown, some rather violet.

The Swiss artist, Paul Klee, produced a colour 'wheel' like this. You can see how, for example, the red becomes more and more orange as more yellow is added to it.

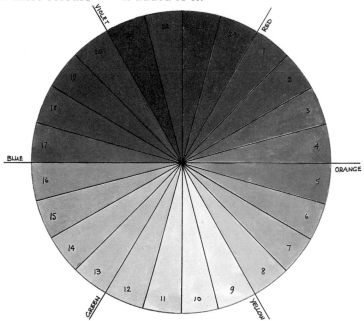

We don't have enough names for all of these colours so, in English, we say, 'that's a very reddish orange' or 'that's an orangey sort of brown'. (We can add 'ish' to red, yellow, green, brown, blue, black and white, and we can add 'y' to red, yellow, green, brown, blue and orange.)

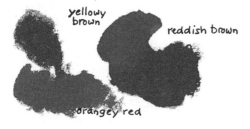

yellowy brown

reddish brown

orangey red

PRIMARY COLOURS

Most people agree that the basic colours for the artist are red, blue and yellow. When you mix these primary colours you can make the secondary colours.

SECONDARY COLOURS

When the primary colours are mixed:
red + yellow = orange
red + blue = purple
yellow + blue = green

TERTIARY COLOURS

When all three primary colours are mixed together you get brown. The kind of brown you get depends on the balance of colours you mix.

COMPLEMENTARY COLOURS

People with reddish hair often wear green clothes. In travel magazines photographers often put people wearing red shirts in the corner of green landscapes. People with blonde hair often wear purple and violet colours. Colours which are opposite to each in the circle are called 'complementary' colours. When complementary colours are seen together they each look richer and more exciting. (Have a look at the wife's green dress and the red bed in van Eyck's picture on page 65. Also look at the small red object in Klee's very green picture on page 73.)

★ Try this experiment. Stare at this red square . . .

After about ten seconds stare at this empty space . . .

Continue to stare at the empty space. Suddenly you will see a coloured, green square appear on the paper (it might not be very clear). It will be the

51

complementary of the red square. There is thus a connection between these complementary colours.

If the artist wants to communicate harmony and peacefulness, he can use colours which are from the same side of the colour wheel. In van Eyck's picture he has painted the husband and the shadows with a similar colour and this gives a gentle feeling.

MATISSE LOVED COLOUR

Look at the painting by Matisse on page 72. Matisse tried to help people to understand how he used colour. He didn't copy each bit of colour he saw in the scene in front of him. He tried to find colours which look good together and which expressed how he felt. Here is what he said about colour:

'Imagine that I am painting a scene in a room. There is a cupboard in front of me: it gives me a feeling like red gives me a feeling . . . so I use red. But when I put the red on the canvas there is a relationship between the red and the white of the canvas. If I make the floor yellow then I choose a yellow which looks right with the red of the cupboard and the white canvas. The colours don't need to look like the colours of the object . . . They must look right together.'

How other artists used colour

Colour is part of the language of the artist. Artists use shape, composition, texture, tone and colour so that they all complement each other. If an artist is concentrating on the decorative character of the subject then the colours as well as the shapes may be more decorative than naturalistic. This applies to Matisse but also to the artist from Basholi whose picture is on page

38. The story he painted is one of the great traditional stories. It is a story without a particular time and place. There was no need for the artist to draw a 'real' house or to use the sort of colours which might exist on a real house. He wanted to use beautiful colours which would please us and communicate his and his society's pleasure in the story.

Hilliard, (see page 61), wanted to show us an individual young man suffering from a broken heart . . . at least for a few moments! The drawing is naturalistic and so is the colour. But in a good painting like this the colour is not only naturalistic. Hilliard has chosen colours which are in harmony together; all the colours are greens and blues, whites and blacks, there is a little bit of brown. There are no contrasting colours as in van Eyck's picture on page 65 and even in Giotto's picture on page 56. Even if a painting is 'naturalistic' the artist must still choose colours which 'work together' and communicate feeling. Pollock and Rothko, (see pages 71 and 77), didn't want to make us recognise anything at all in their pictures. They were completely free to choose colours according to the general feeling they wished to express.

Which colours do you like?

There may be one main colour in a picture . . . perhaps green in a painting of the English countryside by Constable or yellow in van Gogh's painting of sunflowers. If you like green or yellow then you may like their paintings for that reason.

★ Put these colours in the order in which you like them: blue, green, orange, red, violet, yellow.

★★ Ask your friends to do the same and see whether there is a difference according to personality or to sex.

Professor H.J. Eysenk asked 21,060 people for their preferences and found that most people liked the colours in the following order: blue, red, green, violet, orange, yellow.

★★ What do red, blue, yellow, green, purple, orange, brown and black mean to you? And what do they mean to your friends?

Some people say that red is hot, passionate and confident, and they say that green is pleasant and calm. Is colour like a language? Does it mean similar things to many people?

Design and composition

The spot lives!

Here is a spot. Look at it. Doesn't it seem to move? Doesn't it seem to be alive, this little black spot? But it's alone. It's alone in a vast, white space.

If you relax your mind and concentrate on a simple mark you feel it's alive. Normally we are too busy to relax, and there isn't enough time to study the life of a spot!

Oh, there's another little spot!

Have you noticed that you look from spot to spot and back again? You don't let your eye wander across the white space to the right or to the left.

But every mark has life and, most importantly, there is a reaction between marks, which makes you want to look from one mark to another. Look at the drama here:

What's happening? What life and movement do you feel? Can you imagine a story about these spots? Who or what is the spot by itself? Is it a leader? A criminal?

Here is the spot again, with three other shapes in a rectangle.

And again, with three more shapes.

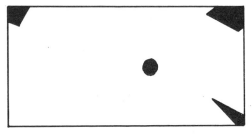

★ Which of the two rectangles do you prefer?

I prefer the first picture. I like the reaction between the shapes because

53

there is a feeling of drama! In the second picture, the black shapes are so small that they have no character and don't give strength to the picture. In the first picture the shapes have character and they give character to the white area as well.

★ Where would you put this 'little character' 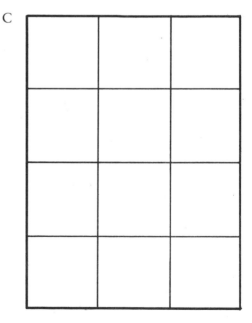 in each of the two compositions above?

★★ If you enjoy arranging these shapes then why not experiment with some of your own and ask other people which they prefer and what they represent.

Boring balance and interesting balance

A

B

★ Which picture do you find the more interesting? Ask as many people as you can to see which picture they prefer.

I have found that most people prefer illustration A. The shape of the bushes in illustration B is the same and they are the same distance from the edge of the picture. The centre of balance of the picture is right in the middle; and this equality seems to be boring.

C

D

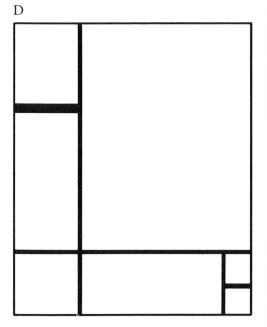

This principle applies to abstract shapes as well. The squares in illustration C are all the same. There is no reason for us to look around the picture; if we have seen one square then we have seen them all. In illustration D the squares are different, each has individual character. We look from one rectangle to the other comparing them and thinking about their relationship. Illustration D is more interesting! When we look at illustration C our eyes don't move; when we look at illustration D our eyes move as they look at each shape.

★★ Try it and notice how your eyes move. Show C and D to a friend. Position yourself so that you can see your friend's eyes. Tell your friend to look at each drawing for a few moments, while you try to guess which one they are looking at by the way their eyes move!

Every picture is made of shapes, spots, lines and spaces. The shapes may be people and roads and trees and skies. They may not represent anything at all. But the arrangement in the picture will always be important. The arrangement can express so many different feelings . . . like music. Matisse said, 'Composition is the art of arranging shapes and colours in order to express the artist's feelings. If part of the picture doesn't contribute to the expression of feeling then it is unnecessary and even bad!'

Giotto and Hokusai control your eyes

COMPOSITION

In Giotto's picture Christ has just been taken down from the cross. His mother, Mary, holds him in her arms and other family and friends stand around him. Christ, the most important person in the picture, is not in the centre. And yet we look at him. The long rock leads our eye to him and several people lean towards him. Mary's dress is very dark and this contrasts with his paleness. (Note the use of tone; see page 45.) But our eye doesn't remain fixed on Christ, it seems to turn round the figures and sometimes moves away up the rock or to the angels above. Notice how important the tree is. The tree is at the top of the rock and stops our eye going up the rock and out of the picture! Similarly the people at the end of the rock and the people standing on the right stop our eye from going out of the picture.

The tree is a symbol for the Tree of

Knowledge. It died when Adam and
Eve left the Garden of Eden. (For more
on symbols see page 64.) We can't
understand symbols unless someone
tells us what they mean. But the
composition in pictures is still a living
language which is there for us to
discover today. And it is this living use
of the language of painting which
makes this 600 year old picture a living
masterpiece today.

*Giotto di Bondone (c. 1266–1337) 'The
Lamentation' (The Arena Chapel, Padua)
This is a fresco painting (see page 14), painted
directly onto the wall of a chapel. Giotto is the
first of the Renaissance artists, and his paintings
show his, and society's, increasing interest in the
individual. (Contrast the illustration of St John
on page 61, which was painted about 150 years
before 'The Lamentation'.) In 'The
Lamentation' the people show emotion, their
positions are different and some even sit with
their back to us (a very new idea in painting!).*

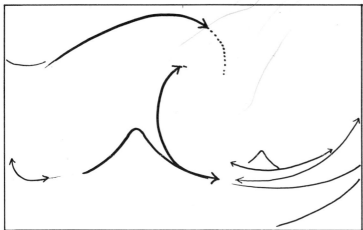

Katsushika Hokusai (1760–1849) 'The Great Wave off Kanagawa' (Metropolitan Museum of Modern Art, New York)
Hokusai liked to be called 'the man who is mad about drawing'! He drew this picture when he was 69 years old. His pictures, and particularly this one, were famous all over Europe. When he was 75 he said, 'When I was six I wanted to paint everything around me. When I was 50 I had already painted many pictures. By the time I
was 73 I had begun to understand the shape of birds, fishes and plants. When I am 100 I will reach a high degree of perfection and when I am 110 everything I draw will be life itself!' Unfortunately he died at the age of 90!

Although Hokusai was taught European perspective he didn't make much use of it. He felt little need for it. See also van Gogh's 'Japanese' painting on page 40.

Six compositions

★ Can you identify these compositions? Each composition is based on a picture in this book.

A

B

D

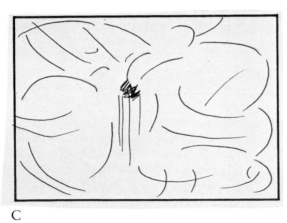

C

E

F

What feelings do these compositions give you? Here are some feelings you might recognise: calm, peaceful, angry, happy, sad, eager, exciting, romantic, emotional, strong, delicate, unhappy.

★ Here are six descriptions of the compositions based on the actual pictures. See if you can match them up correctly. The answers are on page 84.

1 This picture has its own life and power and is not dependent for its strength on the subject. There is a continual twisting movement like flames from the bottom to the top. Sharp angles and curves make our eyes swerve from side to side but the direction is upwards. The contrast of the tones contributes to the feeling of tension and excitement.

2 This is a quiet picture. However, there is a slow and solemn movement between each of the two rectangles. It is not a happy picture but neither is it unhappy; perhaps solemn is the right word?

3 This is a calm picture. However, there is movement in the small, dark shapes on the left, and there is tension in the vertical lines and the pointed shapes.

4 There are strong rectangles here and they are flat across the picture. And yet there is some depth, so the eye goes in and out and across the picture and the mind feels a quiet, confident dignity.

5 There is a strong movement from the right of the picture to the left. And yet the triangle of white points to the right and resists the pull to the left. There is conflict in this pulling to left and right and there is almost no feeling of safety and security in horizontal lines and there are no vertical lines. The shapes seem to be tearing themselves into pieces, and there are small lines which are like cracks in the surface. This is a tense and desperate picture in which life is almost hidden in the darkness.

6 This painting is all about movement! The lines of paint fly in and out like children playing in a school playground. Is it an angry painting or a happy, playful painting? So much depends on your own feeling when you see it!

How to read a picture

Looking at pictures

Art doesn't improve . . . it changes

★ Look at these pictures. When do you think they were painted?

A: 1500 AD   950 AD   18,000 BC
B: 750 BC   100 AD   1972 AD
C: 1920 AD   100 AD   1520 AD
D: 1150 AD   1820 AD   550 BC
E: 80 AD   1588 AD   1755 AD
F: 1906 AD   1234 AD   451 AD

A

B

C

D

E

F

(You will find the answers
on the next page.)

Some people think that art became more and more naturalistic until this century. But did you get the dates right for the pictures? If you did, then you know that naturalistic art and abstract art come and go through the centuries. Art changes just as ideas change. Artists usually reflect the society they are in.

PICTURE A: ABOUT 18,000 BC

France
This picture of a horse was painted on the walls of a cave at Lascaux, in the centre of France. The people of that time hunted horses for food, and were very familiar with horses. (In some pictures the artists used the bumps and hollows of the cave wall to represent the bumps and hollows of the animals' bodies.) Most pictures of animals of this period are very naturalistic. We don't know why the pictures were painted nor, of course, why they were so naturalistic.

PICTURE B: 750 BC

Greece
It is difficult to believe that this very abstract representation isn't modern. In 8th century BC Greece the individual wasn't as important as during the 5th century and in later times. Indeed, in this picture we can't even see that the figure is a woman! We know that it is a woman because it is part of a procession for someone's funeral and the women walked like this with their arms above them. The figure is just one detail taken from a big amphora painted by the Dipylon painter.

PICTURE C: 100 AD

Rome
During Roman times the individual was important. Even the gods were individual, and had their own very human characters. It isn't surprising therefore, that the paintings and the sculpture showed this individuality. After Roman times the individual became less important throughout most of Europe until the Renaissance.

PICTURE D: 1150 AD

Germany
This is a picture of St John the Evangelist. St John isn't shown as an individual; he is a symbol rather than an individual man writing at his desk. The curving, swirling lines and the face are decorative rather than 'real'. The picture is flattened; the artist has shown us the side of the seat and table leg but the top of the holy book. Why does he write with both hands? I don't know. Any ideas?

PICTURE E: 1588 AD

England
This picture is called *Portrait of an Unknown Man*, and it was painted by Nicholas Hilliard. This young man is rich and is wearing fashionable and beautiful clothes. He looks very individual indeed! He isn't happy. He has his hand over his heart, and he feels the pain of love. Although this is a very naturalistic picture there are symbols in it . . . the beauty and the pain of love are symbolised by the flowers and the thorns of the rose. So the picture is painted in a very naturalistic style but, at the same time, the picture must be 'read', the symbols must be understood.

PICTURE F: 1906 AD

France

This painting is called *Les Demoiselles d'Avignon*, and it was painted by Picasso. It was, perhaps, the first great 'cubist' painting. Picasso wanted to create strong shapes. He didn't want to represent the general naturalistic appearance of the women. People who want a general appearance can look at a photograph. It isn't possible to say that this painting, this style or Picasso represent society in Europe in 1906, as there are so many different styles of painting by Picasso and other artists. Perhaps it is this variety of style and expression which represents society rather than any one painting.

Artists today don't usually have important customers who want paintings to represent particular ideas. In recent years rich people have started to buy paintings as an investment as they hope the paintings will become more valuable in the future.

Paintings can become valuable if they are unusual or, better still, unique! Artists today are thus encouraged to experiment and to develop their own special style. The galleries of modern art also encourage this experimental approach. Unfortunately, painting is a language and new languages have to be learned. The result is that many people feel that they can't understand 'modern art' and so they reject it.

A famous painting

Overleaf is the painting by Jan van Eyck showing the marriage of Giovanni Arnolfini and Giovanna Cenami. It is one of the most famous paintings (and no doubt one of the most valuable paintings) in the National Gallery in London. I believe that you can enjoy and appreciate this painting without reading my book about it! And perhaps you should first look at the reproduction and do just that! However, when you have enjoyed looking at it for some time you might like to see if you can answer a few questions about it. The earlier chapters in this book should help you to answer them.

1 How important was the individual person when van Eyck painted this picture?

2 Do you think that the symbolism of painting was important to van Eyck?

3 There are, in fact, a lot of symbols in the picture. Do you know what they mean?

– Why has the man raised his right hand?

– Why are there some figures shown in the mirror?

– What does the candle symbolise?

– What does the little dog symbolise?

– What do the mirror, the crystal beads on the wall and the blue of the woman's sleeves and underskirt symbolise?

– What do the orange and the apple symbolise?

– Why don't Giovanni and Giovanna wear shoes?

4 Can you say which are the most important parts of the picture, which are the second most important parts and which are the least important parts?

5 How does van Eyck make us look at the important parts?

6 What sort of feeling do you get from this picture?

7 How does van Eyck give you this feeling? Look at the colour, the shapes, the tones and the composition.

I have tried to answer these questions, and one or two more.

Jan van Eyck lived in Bruges, Belgium, in the 15th century. Bruges was a rich city and the merchants paid artists to paint pictures of themselves, their families and their success. Giovanni Arnolfini was a rich Italian merchant who bought and sold silk. He lived in Bruges and died there in 1472.

Content of the picture

The painting shows the actual marriage of Giovanni and Giovanna. At that time, in 1434, people didn't have to go to church in order to marry. People could get married when there were other people as witnesses to the important and solemn occasion.

Giovanni and his bride are not wearing shoes because they are showing that the floor is holy ground. Giovanni takes his bride's hand and raises his right hand to show his promise to her. The mirror shows that there are witnesses in the room, and Jan van Eyck has shown that he was there: he has written in Latin on the wall, 'Johannes de Eyck fuit hic', which means 'Jan van Eyck was here'.

There are more symbols in the picture: the single, burning candle symbolises Jesus Christ and the presence of Christ at the marriage. The little dog at the woman's feet symbolises faithfulness. The crystal beads on the wall, the perfect mirror and the blue of the woman's sleeves and underskirt are all symbols of purity. The oranges and the apple may symbolise the innocence of the 'Garden of Eden' in which man and woman were created, according to the Christian bible. Around the mirror

there are ten scenes from the life of Christ and on the high wooden chair next to the bed is a figure, probably of St Margaret, who looked after childbirth.

Form in the picture

The walls, the bed, the floor and all the perspective lines lead us into the room. They invite us to examine the detail of the cloth, the fur, the wood and the glass. However, the perspective lines do more than lead us into the room. They tell us to witness the marriage. The lines on the floor (A) meet together on Giovanni's left wrist. They are saying, 'This man takes this woman to be his wife.' The two lines of the bed at the top of the picture (B) meet on Giovanni's right hand as he commits himself to the marriage. The lines of the ceiling meet on the sentence which van Eyck wrote (C). Finally, the lines of the window point towards Giovanni (D).

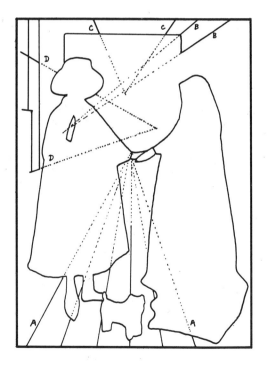

Jan van Eyck (1390–1441) 'The Arnolfini Marriage' (National Gallery, London)

This is one of the first oil paintings in the world and certainly one of the greatest.

According to the rules of perspective, the lines of the floor, wall and ceiling should have met at one point, and they don't! Clearly, van Eyck has used perspective lines as an expression of meaning rather than a technique for representing the appearance of the room.

The organisation of the tones also helps us to read the artist's story. The faces and the hands are the lightest areas. We look from one to the other easily and calmly.

The people, the window, the bed hangings, the carpet, etc. are all vertical . . . and that gives the picture quietness and dignity.

The browns and blacks of the man show his seriousness and, I feel, they relate him to the left hand side of the picture, the floors and walls of the house and the world outside. The green of Giovanna's dress is the complementary colour of the red of the bed, the carpet and the inside of the home. The reds and greens are beautiful together and they connect wife and home.

At first sight this picture looks like a photograph of the past in which we recognise everything we see. However, van Eyck has used symbols, which most people today have never learned. He has also used forms (perspective and colour) to direct our attention and to express feelings.

How did he do it?

What techniques did van Eyck use to paint this wonderful picture? This is an oil painting. Some people think that van Eyck invented oil painting, but others say a German monk, called Theophillus, invented oil painting in 1100.

Van Eyck painted on wood. Two pieces of oak were glued together.

Glue and chalk were painted on the front.

The back of the wood was painted as well. This stops damp getting into the wood and making it bend.

Next van Eyck drew the picture in line.

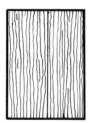

He covered the drawing with a drying oil.

Then he painted a thin colour.

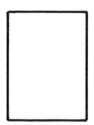

He added a richer colour.

And finally he painted the shadows to give space and volume.

Van Eyck may not have invented oil painting but he was the first great master of it. Technically, his painting is perfect . . . it is still perfect after 600 years.

Van Eyck first painted the light colours, and then added the dark colours. The paint is thinner in the light areas than in the dark areas, but all the paint is quite thin. The richness of the colour comes from the colours in the first layer shining through the thin layers of colour on top. In the woman's face, for example, the white bottom layer of paint shines through the pinks and browns.

Van Eyck painted a picture which we feel we can understand and enjoy.

However, he also chose shapes, colours, tones and composition which give the painting a life of its own. This painting is not just a clever copy of a real scene. In this sense he was concerned with form like a modern painter. I wonder whether any modern paintings will last for 600 years and still look as rich and perfect as *The Arnolfini Marriage*.

Modern art

★ What do you think of modern art? Do you agree with any of these comments?

One point of view?

For 500 years artists painted pictures from a single point of view. At the beginning of the 20th century artists felt free to represent different views of objects and scenes together in a single picture.

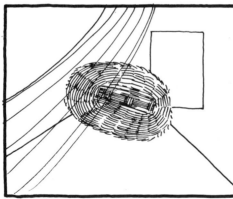

In the first picture above I have drawn all the objects from one position. In the second picture I have drawn each object from a different point of view. I have shown the bottom of the basket because it is a lovely shape and it is very characteristic of the basket. The table is a more interesting shape when we see it from higher up . . . so I have drawn the table from a different angle.

The rectangle of the window is a powerful shape so I have included that as well. I have tried to arrange the shapes and tones in a way which pleases me.

★ Look at an object in front of you, perhaps a pen, a cup or a radio. How many different shapes can you find in each one? You might even like to try drawing them and arranging them in a way which pleases you.

Here are some shapes which I found in the objects in front of me on my table.

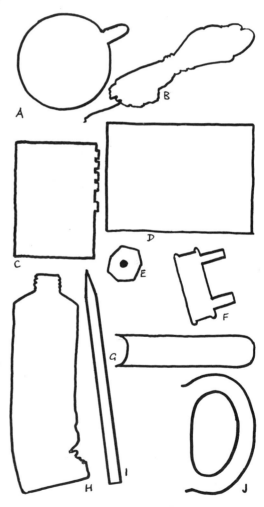

Can you match up the descriptions with the drawings?

1 A handle of a cup seen from the side
2 A cup seen from the top
3 A pencil seen from behind
4 A small cassette tape recorder
5 A book open and seen from above
6 A book closed and seen from the side

What do you think the mystery objects are?

Here is my arrangement of them.

Warning! Artists like Matisse would be critical of the ideas described above! Matisse would say that you must be inspired by feeling, a poetic feeling, and you should not just make a pleasing, decorative arrangement.

Different 'languages'

As you look at the next few pages you will see that the artists have been expressing different ideas and using the language of painting in very different ways. You can either concentrate on the ideas and the 'painting languages' you know or you can try to understand new languages and new ideas. But it takes time, energy and determination to learn a new language! The best way to learn a foreign language is to listen to it as much as you can (and to speak it!) . . . and the best way to begin to understand and to appreciate paintings which are new to you is to look at them very often and to be open to new ideas.

★★ Look for the different and conflicting ideas expressed by the following artists.

RENÉ MAGRITTE

I like this painting. It doesn't make me happy, but it makes me feel the strangeness of time. At the moment, you are reading this book and you are probably sitting down. When you have finished reading you will stand up and go away. The seat will be empty. It will remain there, after you have gone. The empty chair, the old shoes, the

69

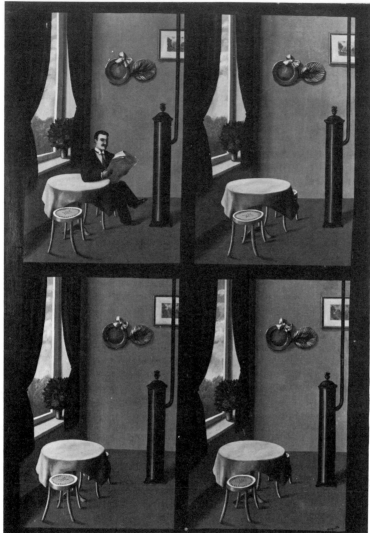

*René Magritte (1898–
1967) 'Man with a
Newspaper' (Tate
Gallery, London)*

doorway, the window in Magritte's picture make me think of time past as much as time present. Time flies, it runs like water, like air through our fingers. Magritte, for me, represents how little I understand. He painted ordinary objects and scenes and he shows us how we don't understand even these. We think we know them but we never really think about them!

Magritte lived with his wife in an ordinary house in an ordinary suburb of Brussels for 30 years. He didn't want to mix with the artistic and intellectual world. He didn't like people who wanted to make theories about his pictures. He said, 'One cannot speak about mystery. One must be seized by it.'

Magritte is warning us that it isn't always possible to translate ideas from one language to another. I have tried to describe my feelings about Magritte's picture. I hope he wouldn't think that these were useless theories!

JACKSON POLLOCK

Jackson Pollock dripped and threw paint onto his pictures, which were often on the floor. He said, 'On the floor, I am at ease. I feel nearer, more a part of the painting. I can walk around it. I can work from all four sides. I can feel that I am in the painting.'

Pollock liked physical action. He swung and moved as though he was dancing. Because he stood over his painting he could move from his hips rather than from his shoulders. He created the dancing lines which weave in and out; these lines make rhythms across the surface.

Pollock obviously didn't want to represent objects, people and scenes. He wanted to make an object with character – a painting.

Jackson Pollock (1912–1956) 'Yellow Islands'
(Tate Gallery, London)

I TAKE FROM NATURE WHAT I NEED.

Henri Matisse (1869–1954) 'Music' (Albright-Knox Art Gallery, Buffalo)
Henri Matisse liked to paint people more than anything else. His paintings are delightful; the shapes have rhythm and the colours become

alive against each other. They don't threaten us. Contrast Munch on page 24 and Bacon on page 74.) And for more ideas on the paintings of Matisse see page 52.

HENRI MATISSE

Henri Matisse is famous for the wonderful colours of his paintings and for their pleasing, decorative effect. In an interview in 1952, Matisse said: 'First of all, I must say that there is no single abstract art. If the subject of a painting isn't important, if there is no story in the picture, then it is abstract. Today the artist doesn't need to represent objects. However, even though he has to concentrate on the picture he must remember the object and his feelings for the object. One starts with the object, then the feelings follow. One doesn't start from nothing. Today, too many so-called abstract painters start from nothing and so they arrive at nothing. They have no strength, no inspiration, no feeling. One doesn't find any expression of feeling in their colours. They don't relate their colours to each other. If they can't create relationships they are using colours uselessly. The French word "rapport" means the connection between things. "Rapport" is love. Without "rapport", without love, there is no way of choosing what to do. Without love there is no art.'

Matisse shows us in this interview that

he wanted to paint colours and shapes which are related to each other rather than to object and scenes. He wanted to express feelings and didn't want to describe objects in a photographic way. Most artists since 1900 have had a similar aim.

PAUL KLEE

Klee had many interesting ideas about painting. He was a teacher and he wrote many books. He thought that every colour, shape, line and texture had its own life and character, and he wanted these characters to live in his paintings.

He wanted to paint reality but not the reality which we see outside ourselves. He wanted to paint the very real feelings and ideas which he experienced within himself, so he searched for metaphors and symbols to represent the inside reality.

This picture shows a fashionable, young woman. She is surrounded by

*Paul Klee (1879–1940)
'A Girl's Adventure'
(Tate Gallery,
London)*

NOWADAYS WE ARE CONCERNED ABOUT REALITY AND WE ARE NOT CONCERNED ABOUT THE MERELY VISIBLE!

unpleasant spirits and she can do nothing about them. The evil bird is taking hold of her and perhaps the arrow is going to attack her like a snake. The main colour in the picture is green, a dark, olive green. Some of the small shapes are red, the complementary colour and also the colour of action and of life.

How does this picture make you feel? You may not be able to describe your feelings in words . . . that is understandable. After all, this is the language of painting and we can't always translate ideas easily from one language to another.

FRANCIS BACON

Francis Bacon once told a BBC interviewer, 'I have nothing to express.' However, for many people who look at his pictures, Bacon expresses horror, loneliness, violence and oppression. There is no love in these paintings. The people don't have a warm and a

Francis Bacon (b. 1909) 'Triptych 1971' central panel (Private Collection, New York)
Each of the three panels in the triptych is 147.5 cm wide and 198 cm high.

I HAVE ALWAYS BEEN VERY AFFECTED BY PICTURES OF SLAUGHTER HOUSES AND MEAT. THEY BELONG, VERY MUCH, TO THE CRUCIFIXION OF CHRIST.

friendly spirit. They are trapped and desperate animals rather than people. Sometimes the paint is smeared across the picture and expresses anger and violence, but the subject might be love making . . . or is it fighting?

Francis Bacon doesn't want to show us angry people. He wants to show us angry paint! Then we will feel anger and not just see it. (In a similar way, the quality of the voice in anger is more important than the words themselves.) Paint, of course, can't be angry! However, lines and shapes can express anger and it is lines of this kind which fill Bacon's pictures. Compare the lines and movement in Bacon's picture with the picture by van de Velde on page 24, and indeed many other pictures in the book.

Bacon says that art used to be an expression of religion and artists had hope through religion. Now, he says, we have no religion and artists have no hope. Art is a game. Artists concentrate on the game and don't have to think about the awful unknown.

In one important way Francis Bacon is a traditional painter. His paintings are seen more or less from one viewpoint. And it is true that he is more concerned with expressing feeling than he is with telling a story which is quite clear and can be put into words.

FERNAND LEGER

Leger was a socialist and he wanted his paintings to teach people. He wanted a society in which people get along together as smoothly as machines. His paintings show smooth, gentle, but strong shapes.

Leger liked machines. During the First World War he began to admire the power and efficiency of machinery. At the same time he began to admire and respect the character of the French soldiers. 'In the war I got to know the French people; my companions were miners, road menders, metal and woodworkers. I admired their sense of reality and practicality. More than that, however, I discovered that they were poets! They were inventors of everyday, poetic images.'

Leger wasn't an abstract artist, because he wanted us to recognise the

objects he painted. Nevertheless, he wanted to create colours and shapes which had a life and character of their own, so his paintings are not just illustrations like photographs.

Fernand Leger (1881–1955) 'Two Women Holding Flowers' (Tate Gallery, London)

MARK ROTHKO

Rothko's paintings are very big. He said, 'I want to be intimate and human. If you paint a small picture you are outside it and you control it. If you paint a big picture you are in it.' However, I don't agree that we remain outside a smaller picture. (See the van Eyck on page 65.)

Rothko liked tragic and timeless subjects. He painted large areas of colour with soft edges. His paintings are like landscapes with huge areas of sky and land . . . but, of course, there is no detail; there are no trees and buildings, there are no clouds and birds. Before 1957 he painted light, bright pictures, but then he began to use dark colours. He felt his paintings had a religious meaning, and he wanted to affect people. He didn't want to paint 'social' paintings like Leger, but to paint beautiful and eternal symbols. (Mark Rothko killed himself in 1970.)

Mark Rothko (1903–1970) 'Light Red Over Black' (Tate Gallery, London)

THE SHAPES IN THE PICTURE ARE ACTORS WHO MOVE FREELY AND WITHOUT SHAME.

Rothko and Pollock are sometimes called 'non-representational' painters: they didn't want to make things recognisable in their pictures. However, they used very different language forms: Rothko used calm shapes and colour combinations, and Pollock used wild, excited shapes, lines, colours and tones.

How to judge a picture

Your collection of pictures

★ Just imagine . . . if you could have five of the pictures reproduced in this book and have them in your own home, which would you choose?

1 If you wanted a cheerful, pleasing painting for your living room.

2 If you wanted a painting to express order, balance and stillness.

3 If you wanted a painting to remind you of the richness of human nature.

4 If you wanted a painting to convey excitement and passion.

5 If you could choose one more painting for your collection which one would it be? And why would you choose that one?

★★ Ask a friend what he or she would choose.

Form and content in painting

You may like a painting because you like the subject: the subject may be a favourite holiday place, a romantic person or a lovely bunch of flowers. But then it isn't the painting that you like, it is the subject! Cézanne said, 'Give me some firewood and I will give you a painting.' He meant that the subject or content of the picture is without importance.

If we are judging the painting then surely this is true. We have all seen weak or even bad paintings of beautiful things. I would rather have a painting of firewood by Cézanne than a characterless painting of a beautiful person or place by someone else!

So what is a weak or even a bad painting? In the next sections I will describe some of the things which I think make a bad painting.

Characterless forms

In each of the earlier sections of this book I have described how artists try to give character and feeling to the forms they use. It is more important that an artist uses colours which relate to each other than to the object they are representing. It is more important that the shapes the artist uses communicate his feelings than represent the exact appearance of the object or scene he is painting. It is important that the tones give importance and order to the picture. Above all, the composition, which is the combination, arrangement and relationship of all the shapes, colours, tones and textures must be strong and full of character.

Is detail important?

People often say, 'Isn't it marvellous! Look at all the detail. It must have taken hours of work.' I don't think hard work is a sign of a good picture. Hard work in itself isn't important. It is only important if it is done to achieve something. If the forms are weak then the painting is weak, even though the painting is full of careful detail and the artist has spent his whole life on it. Isn't it boring if someone describes every detail of their holiday to you? However, it isn't boring if there is delight in the detail which expresses their joy.

Van Eyck painted detail in *The Arnolfini Marriage* (page 65), but the main forms are full of character. The detail gives an extra quality of concentration and care.

Matisse said, 'In the bad periods of art, artists were interested in details and small forms. In the great periods of art, artists were interested in the main character of big shapes and their relationships.'

Isn't he clever?

Some artists want to show how easily they can paint the reflections in a river or give an impression of sunshine on Mediterranean houses. They use their palette knife and flick and smear the paint across the canvas. It takes practice to learn how to do this, but is it 'good'? If you admire such skill then you will, no doubt, feel that the painting is good. However, artists who want to appear technically clever are often less concerned with the character and strength of the painting as a whole. If one is familiar with the language of painting then one can see that such technical skill isn't worth much. A shiny door knob doesn't mean a house with good foundations. A few clever remarks don't mean an intelligent brain . . . except to the innocent person!

The painting by van der Vaart of the violin on page 12 is very clever but it doesn't have strong qualities of composition and it doesn't communicate feeling. It isn't a 'great' painting for this reason.

Delacroix, the great French artist, criticised Carracci, the Italian artist. He said:

THE CLEVERNESS IN HIS PAINTINGS IS MORE POWERFUL THAN THE FEELING. HIS TECHNIQUE IS THE MOST IMPORTANT CHARACTERISTIC OF HIS PAINTINGS. HE KNOWS TOO MUCH ABOUT TECHNIQUE AND HE DOESN'T STUDY, SO HE NO LONGER DISCOVERS ANYTHING NEW OR INTERESTING !

EUGENE DELACROIX (1798-1863)

AGOSTINO CARRACCI (1560-1609)

But Delacroix liked Leonardo!

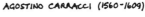

I DON'T THINK ABOUT THE TECHNIQUE IN LEONARDO'S PAINTINGS. ONLY THE FEELING REACHES MY MIND.

LEONARDO DA VINCI (1452-1519)

£7,200,000! Is it worth it?

Some painters are considered great, and
their paintings are very expensive to
buy. It is a big moment when a great
work of art comes up for sale.

£7.2 million for 'Seascape' by Turner

$6.4 million for 'Juliet and her nurse' by Turner

$5.4 million for 'Juan de Pareja' by Velasquez

$5.3 million for 'Self Portrait' by Picasso

$5.2 million for 'The Poet's Garden' by van Gogh

$6 million for three paintings by Jackson Pollock

In the 1970s the prices of paintings rose
rapidly. The galleries and salerooms,
like Sotheby's in Bond Street, London,
worked very hard! As a result rich
people and institutions believed that art
was a good investment. Paintings are
now judged by their cost and not by
what they communicate. You buy a
painting, hang it on the wall and watch
it grow in value. When a painting has
just been bought for a lot of money by
an art gallery, crowds of people want
to see it. Later, people forget and fewer
people wish to see it.

There is a strange story about an art
object by Joseph Beuys, the German
artist, which was in a museum . . . it
was a child's bath tub on a stand.
There was a party in the museum and
the people at the party filled the bath
tub with cold water and put bottles of
beer in it to keep them cool. No
damage was done, however the owner
of Beuys's bath tub took the museum to
court and was awarded $94,000. Beuys
was very happy and said it was a
victory over the selfishness of beer
drinkers.

This story shows that art is business
today.

Here is one of mine!

Andrew Wright (b. 1937) 'Floods in Normandy'

This is a watercolour painting on paper. Watercolours are a favourite medium for English artists and have been for a long time. (In this book there are two other English watercolour paintings, one by Nicholas Hilliard on page 61 and one by John Sell Cotman on page 47.)

This is a painting of flooded fields. The sky promises more rain; there is a feeling of threat from the clouds which are generally darker than the water. The wetness of the watercolour expresses very usefully the wetness of the weather! Although the brush strokes were put down quickly I hope you will feel that the composition is quite strong. I have tried to give characterful shape to the bank and buildings in the middle and I have tried to give firm direction to the tree trunks and branches.

In watercolour painting the paper is used to show the white areas . . . the artist doesn't use white paint. It is quite common to let several areas of white paper show through. This gives a busy, restless feeling to the painting as well as a feeling of the shining wetness of a wet day.

Last thoughts

The language of painting and the language of words are similar. In paintings or in words we can represent people, actions, events and ideas and we can express feelings of calmness, anger, excitement, joy, dignity and sorrow: we can express the feeling of the moment and the idea of eternity.

We are used to choosing words which are appropriate for our intentions. Everyone speaks but not everyone paints. And for this reason most people are not so familiar with painting. I hope that this book will have helped you to appreciate and enjoy the variety of languages of painting a little more.

Answers

Page 4

Looking at Hogarth's picture from left to right and top to bottom I can find 14 mistakes or deliberate tricks:
– the water is sloping
– we can see on top of the church tower but we look directly at the church and we can see both ends of the church
– the end of the church is in the water
– the crow is enormous, it is half the size of the tree
– the line of trees leading to the crow's tree gets larger as it goes into the distance rather than smaller
– the trees at the beginning of the line pass in front of the sign board of the inn
– the sign board of the inn is supported on two buildings
– the woman leans out of the window and lights the pipe of the man on the hill
– on the bridge the front horse goes behind the tree which is on the hillside behind the bridge
– the man in the boat shoots at the swan on the other side of the bridge (he wouldn't be able to see it from that position)
– the cows on the road are probably all mature and yet they get bigger as they go away from us
– the man fishing at the front of the picture is holding his rod over and beyond the rod of the other fisherman
– we can see the tops and the bottoms

of the barrels at the front of the picture at the same time (note the perspective drawing on all the buildings is peculiar!)

– the man at the front is supposed to be standing on a flat tiled floor and yet it seems to be more like a vertical wall

Page 11

Hobbema was interested in space and the character of trees.

Van der Weyden expressed dignity, beauty and quietness.

Turner loved light and colour.

The artist from Basholi wanted to tell a story and liked rich patterns.

De Hooch valued the expensive quality of houses, furniture and clothes.

Uccello liked complicated patterns of shapes.

Page 18

This is Rudolph Arnheim's analysis of the shapes:

Page 26

I am thinking about:
1 Leger, page 76
2 Van der Weyden, page 25
3 Klee, page 73
4 St John, page 61
5 Rembrandt, page 43
6 Munch, page 24

Page 37

A3 Monet, page 8
B4 De Hooch, page 23
C1 Hobbema, page 36
D2 Giotto, page 56

Page 47

Here is my analysis of the tonal areas in Cotman's painting.

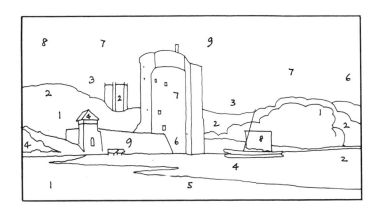

Page 48

Here is my analysis of the tonal areas in Goya's picture.

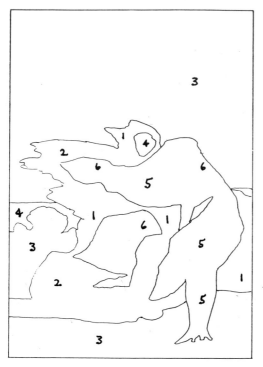

Page 49

The four texts describe:
1 Canaletto, page 9
2 Fragonard, page 23
3 Hokusai, page 57
4 Leger, page 76

Page 59

A5 Goya *A Stormy Night*, page 48
B4 De Hooch *A Boy Bringing Pomegranates*, page 23
C6 Pollock *Yellow Islands*, page 71
D2 Rothko *Light Red Over Black*, page 77
E1 Picasso *Les Demoiselles d'Avignon*, page 61
F3 Monet *The Thames Below Westminster*, page 8

Acknowledgements

The author and publishers are grateful to the following institutions who have given permission for paintings, photographs and texts to be reproduced:

Faber and Faber Ltd for the extract on p. 2 from 'The Thought Fox' from *Hawk in the Rain* by Ted Hughes; 'The Frontispiece to Kirby's Perspective' by William Hogarth on p. 3, 'Crucifixion' by Robert de Lisle on p. 32 and 'A Stormy Night' by Francisco Goya on p. 48 are reproduced by courtesy of the Trustees of the British Museum; The Los Angeles County Museum of Art and ADAGP 1985 for 'La Trahison des Images (Ceci n'est pas une pipe)' by René Magritte on p. 4, purchased with funds provided by the Mr and Mrs William Preston Harrison Collection; 'The Thames Below Westminster' by Claude Monet on p. 8, 'The Fighting Temeraire' by J. M. W. Turner on p. 16, 'Portrait of a Lady' by Rogier van der Weyden on p. 25, 'The Battle of San Romano' by Paolo Uccello on p. 34, 'The Avenue, Middleharnis' by Meyndert Hobbema on p. 36, 'The Annunciation' by Carlo Crivelli on p. 38, 'Self-Portrait' by Paul Cézanne on p. 43, and 'The Arnolfini Marriage' by Jan van Eyck on p. 65 are reproduced by courtesy of the Trustees, The National Gallery, London; 'The Doge's Palace and Riva degli Schiavoni' by Antonio Canaletto on p. 9, 'The Swing' by Jean-Honoré Fragonard on p. 23, 'A Boy Bringing Pomegranates' by Pieter de Hooch on p. 23, 'Ships in a Calm' by Willem van de Velde on p. 24, and 'The Artist's Son Titus' by Rembrandt van Rijn on p. 43 are reproduced by permission of the Trustees of the Wallace Collection; Madame Tussauds and Linda Tunstall for the photograph on p. 11; 'Violin' by Jan van der Vaart on p. 12 is reproduced by permission of the Chatsworth House Trust; 'The Scream' by Edvard Munch on p. 24 is reproduced by permission of the National Gallery, Oslo; Paul Klee Foundation, Museum of Fine Arts, Berne and Cosmopress Geneva and ADAGP Paris 1985 for 'Low Tide' on p. 28 and 'Storm Spirit' and 'Lost in Thought' on p. 29 by Paul Klee; 'Resourceful Radha' by a painter from Basholi in the Punjab on p. 38, and 'Portrait of an Unknown Man' by Nicholas Hilliard on p. 61 are reproduced by courtesy of the Board of Trustees of the Victoria and Albert; the Tate Gallery, London for 'The Gardener Vallier' by Paul Cézanne on p. 40, (and DACS 1985) for 'Seated Nude' by Pablo Picasso on p. 41, (and ADAGP 1985) for 'Man with a Newspaper' by René Magritte on p. 70, 'Yellow Islands' by Jackson Pollock on p. 71, (and Cosmopress Geneva and ADAGP Paris 1985) for 'A Girl's Adventure' by Paul Klee on p. 73, (and DACS 1985) for 'Two Women Holding Flowers' by Fernand Leger on p. 76, and 'Light Red Over Black' by Mark Rothko on p. 77; National Museum Vincent van Gogh, Amsterdam for 'Flowering Plum Tree' by Vincent van Gogh on p. 40; Whitworth Art Gallery, University of Manchester for 'The Water Tower, York' by J. S. Cotman on p. 47; Archivi Alinari and Scala/Firenze for 'The Lamentation' by Giotto di Bondone on p. 14 and p. 56; The Metropolitan Museum of Art, The Howard Mansfield Collection, Rogers Fund 1936 for 'The Great Wave off Kanagawa' by Katsushika Hokusai on p. 57; Ray Delvert and DACS 1985 for the Lascaux photograph on p. 60; the National Archaeological Museum, Athens for the detail of the Attic Geometric amphora on p. 60; Hessisches Landesmuseum, Darmstadt for the miniature of St John the Evangelist on p. 61; The Museum of Modern Art, the Lillie P. Bliss Bequest and DACS 1985 for 'Les Demoiselles d'Avignon' by Pablo Picasso on p. 61; Albright-Knox Art Gallery, Buffalo, New York and DACS 1985 for 'La Musique' by Henri Matisse on p. 72; a private collection for 'Triptych 1971' by Francis Bacon on pp. 74–5.

The photograph on p. 11 is by Linda Tunstall; the other photographs are by the author.

Index of paintings